Hidden Depths: The Kincaid Conspiracy and The Secrets of The Grand Canyon

Cassiel E. Nox

Published by Cassiel E. Nox, 2024.

While every precaution has been taken in the preparation of this book, the publisher assumes no responsibility for errors or omissions, or for damages resulting from the use of the information contained herein.

HIDDEN DEPTHS: THE KINCAID CONSPIRACY AND THE SECRETS OF THE GRAND CANYON

First edition. September 17, 2024.

ISBN: 979-8224867219

Written by Cassiel E. Nox.

Also by Cassiel E. Nox

From Roswell to Today: The Timeline of UFOs and Aliens

The Hidden Tunnels: Unraveling the Enigmatic Secrets of the Denver Airport

Christopher Columbus: The Untold Story of Discovery and Controversy

Hidden Depths: The Kincaid Conspiracy and The Secrets of The Grand Canyon

Table of Contents

Hidden Depths: The Kincaid Conspiracy and The Secrets of The Grand

Part I: Unveiling the Mystery

The Haunting Silence of the Canyon

Deep within the heart of the Grand Canyon lies a mystery that has captivated the imagination of explorers and researchers for generations. The towering cliffs and serpentine canyons hold secrets whispered only by the wind, echoing through the ages. As one stands at the precipice of this natural wonder, a haunting silence descends as if the very stones themselves are guarding the truth from prying eyes.

The Grand Canyon, carved by the relentless forces of nature over millions of years, is a testament to the power of time and the enduring mysteries of the Earth. Its rugged beauty and vast expanse have drawn countless adventurers, each seeking to unravel the enigmas hidden within its depths. But one mystery stands above the rest: a tale of an explorer named G.E. Kincaid and his astonishing discovery that challenges everything we know about the canyon's history.

Whispers of Ancient Civilizations

In the early 20th century, rumors about an ancient civilization hiding in the Grand Canyon started spreading. That is where G.E. Kincaid's story begins. Kincaid, an intrepid explorer with an insatiable curiosity, heard these whispers and felt compelled to investigate. Armed with little more than his wits and a burning desire for knowledge, he set out to uncover the truth behind these tantalizing rumors.

As Kincaid delved deeper into the canyon's secrets, he stumbled upon something that would forever change the course of history. In a remote canyon region, he discovered a series of caves and tunnels that were the work of an advanced ancient civilization. The walls had these crazy carvings and hieroglyphs that Kincaid had never seen before.

The implications of this discovery were staggering. If Kincaid's findings were factual, it would mean that a sophisticated society had thrived in the Grand Canyon long before conventional history suggested. The possibility of a lost civilization hidden beneath the canyon's rugged exterior was thrilling and terrifying, challenging everything we thought we knew about the region's past.

The Lost Explorers and Their Secrets

News of Kincaid's finding spread like wildfire, attracting other explorers and researchers to the Grand Canyon, each hoping to unravel the mysteries of that ancient civilization. Unfortunately, the canyon's brutal landscape and the secrets they sought led to the demise of countless daring explorers who mysteriously vanished.

The disappearances only fueled the growing conspiracy surrounding Kincaid's findings. People whispered about spooky curses and spirits guarding the lost civilization's treasures, and others mentioned secret organizations trying to hide the truth. As time passed, the legend of the lost civilization in the Grand Canyon became more intriguing, drawing in those daring enough to uncover its mysteries.

Echoes of a Forgotten Past

As the 21st century dawned, the mystery of Kincaid's discovery in the Grand Canyon remained as perplexing as ever. Despite the passing of time, the lost civilization's allure continued to captivate researchers and adventurers. The echoes of the past whisper secrets in the canyon.

Driven by curiosity, brave explorers embarked on a years-long journey to recreate Kincaid's legendary odyssey, uncover the secrets of the hidden caves, and navigate the intricate tunnel system he meticulously documented. The arduous and dangerous nature of the canyon became apparent as they faced the unforgiving terrain and vastness. A sense of disappointment filled the air as countless people walked away empty-handed. The canyon remained tight-lipped, refusing to reveal its hidden wonders.

Cryptic Symbols Carved in Stone

Among the most intriguing aspects of Kincaid's alleged discovery were the cryptic symbols and hieroglyphs he claimed to have found within the hidden caves. These enigmatic carvings, etched into the stone with meticulous precision, hinted at a language and a culture far removed from anything known to modern civilization.

Researchers and linguists pored over the limited sketches and descriptions left behind by Kincaid, attempting to decipher the meaning behind the strange symbols. People guessed the hieroglyphs were ancient writing from a lost civilization. Others believed the symbols held a more esoteric purpose, encoding secrets of the universe or serving as a gateway to otherworldly realms.

As the study of the cryptic symbols intensified, people grew more convinced that the key to understanding the Grand Canyon's lost civilization lay hidden within these enigmatic carvings. The race to unlock their secrets became a driving force behind the ongoing search for Kincaid's elusive caves, fueling the fires of conspiracy and drawing more seekers into the canyon's depths.

Echoes of a Forgotten Past

As the 21st century dawned, the mystery of Kincaid's discovery in the Grand Canyon continued to baffle researchers, adding to its enigmatic allure. The passage of time did nothing to diminish the captivating allure of the lost civilization, which continued to fascinate researchers and adventurers. The echoes of this forgotten past reverberated off the canyon walls, whispering long-lost secrets and untold truths.

Adventurers tried to follow Kincaid's path, hoping to find the mysterious caves and tunnels he had described. However, the harsh landscape and the enormity of the canyon made exploration difficult and dangerous. No one returned with anything, and the canyon hid its secrets.

The past continued to hold intrigue. Clues kept appearing, fueling curiosity about a lost history. The ancient symbols and hieroglyphs carved on the canyon's walls seemed to have the key to the truth, but their meanings remained unclear.

Cryptic Symbols Carved in Stone

Kincaid's discovery was fascinating because of the weird symbols and hieroglyphs he said he found in the secret caves. These carvings, made with great skill, suggested a language and culture quite different from anything known today. Experts and linguists tried to determine what the symbols meant from Kincaid's sketches and notes. The hieroglyphs from a forgotten civilization had old secrets that sparked the imagination. Others said the symbols were about mysterious things, like hidden secrets and magic places.

A bunch of people thought the mysterious symbols had the answer to the lost civilization of the Grand Canyon. They wanted to discover their secrets and kept looking for Kincaid's hidden caves, stirring up conspiracy and attracting more explorers to the canyon.

The Descent into Darkness

The journey was tiresome for those courageous enough to venture into the Grand Canyon's uncharted territories in search of Kincaid's discovery. The descent into the canyon's depths was a harrowing experience, a plunge into a world of shadows and secrets where the line between reality and legend blurred.

Navigating treacherous paths, the seekers of truth skirted along narrow ledges and descended into abyssal chasms where the sun's light dared not reach. With every passing moment, the canyon's twisted geography seemed to morph and transform as if it had a secret to keep.

In the suffocating darkness of the canyon's depths, the explorers confronted the terrain's physical challenges and the psychological toll of the unknown. The weight of the centuries pressed down upon them, and the whispers of the past grew louder with each step they took. People talked about seeing weird things and spooky ghost figures that would appear and disappear in the cave shadows.

The darkness kept closing in, and the air felt heavy with the weight of the past. As they dug deeper, they started questioning Kincaid's discovery and what those who wanted to hide it were up to. Mortals were not meant to see the secrets of the Grand Canyon, and the price of finding them out could be significantly more than anyone ever thought.

Ghostly Encounters Along the Rim

As exploring the Grand Canyon's hidden secrets continued, strange reports surfaced from those who ventured along the canyon's rim. Hikers and campers spoke of ghostly encounters and unexplained phenomena, fueling the growing sense of unease surrounding Kincaid's discovery.

As the sun dipped below the horizon, whispers of spooky figures haunting the canyon spread among the locals. Others reported hearing disembodied voices echoing through the wind, whispering in languages long forgotten by the modern world. The canyon had this crazy energy, like the ancient spirits were waking up.

As the tales of ghostly encounters spread, the boundary between myth and reality blurred. Were these sightings merely the products of overactive imaginations fueled by the legend of Kincaid's discovery? Or was something more sinister at play, a supernatural force that sought to guard the secrets of the lost civilization from prying eyes?

Veiled Clues in the Hidden Caverns

Despite our efforts, we could not locate Kincaid's caves. However, our exploration led us to discover concealed chambers deep within the Grand Canyon. These underground spaces, isolated from the external world for an extended period, contained intriguing evidence that suggested a long-lost civilization.

Explorers who dared to venture into these hidden caverns found themselves in a labyrinth of twisting passages and underground chambers, each more enigmatic than the last. The walls were all decked out with excellent pictures. Their colors remained vibrant despite the passing of countless centuries. The depictions highlighted scenes of ancient people freezing their customs and living in time upon the stone.

The explorers kept going in the caves and found all these weird artifacts and relics. Finding strange things made with unknown materials hinted at an ancient civilization being more advanced than we thought. The findings were mind-blowing, proving that the lost city's people had ancient knowledge and skills.

Yet, for every clue uncovered, new questions arose. The hidden caverns were part of a more extensive network, a vast underground city that stretched far beyond the boundaries of the known canyon. The extent of the lost civilization's reach remained a mystery, requiring a lifetime of exploration.

Enigmatic Hieroglyphs and Puzzling Petroglyphs

As the exploration of the Grand Canyon's hidden depths continued, the enigmatic hieroglyphs and puzzling petroglyphs found within the caverns and caves became the focus of intense study. These cryptic symbols, etched into the fabric of the canyon's walls, held the promise of unlocking the secrets of the lost civilization.

Teams of linguists, archaeologists, and cryptographers pored over the ancient markings, attempting to decipher their meaning. The hieroglyphs were a pain to decipher because they had a complex writing system like other ancient scripts. The petroglyphs depicted scenes and figures that hinted at a rich mythological tradition, a glimpse into the beliefs and stories of a people who had long vanished from the Earth.

As the study of hieroglyphs and petroglyphs progressed, patterns emerged. Certain symbols repeated themselves across different sites, suggesting a common language or cultural connection. Yet, the true meaning behind these enigmatic markings remained in mystery, their secrets jealously guarded by passing time.

Experts have thought that the hieroglyphs and petroglyphs in the Grand Canyon contain the secrets of ancient civilization and humanity. These mysterious symbols contain hidden knowledge that solves the puzzles of the cosmos.

Unraveling the Threads of Time and Truth

As the exploration of the Grand Canyon's mysteries deepened, the threads of time and truth intertwined in more complex patterns. The search for Kincaid's lost discovery had opened Pandora's box of secrets that threatened to unravel the fabric of our understanding of the past.

The Enigmatic Grand Canyon

The Whispering Wind: An Introduction to Ancient Secrets

A natural wonder lies in the heart of the American Southwest, captivating the imagination of humanity for generations. The Grand Canyon is a fantastic display of nature's strength and beauty. This thing is alive and full of mysteries we have not figured out yet.

As the wind whispers through the canyon's crevices, carrying with it the echoes of a forgotten past, one cannot help but feel a sense of awe and wonder. The air seems charged with an energy that defies explanation as if the spirits of those who once walked these ancient lands still linger, waiting to share their stories with those willing to listen.

A Silent Observer: The Unseen Forces at Play

For centuries, the Grand Canyon has stood as a silent observer, bearing witness to the rise and fall of civilizations, passing time, and the endless cycle of life and death. Its walls have seen the footsteps of countless generations, from the ancient Indigenous peoples who called this land home to the modern-day adventurers who seek to unravel its mysteries.

Yet, the canyon is more than just a passive observer. There are unseen forces at play, a hidden energy that pulses through the rock and the river, shaping the very essence of this place. The canyon is alive as if it has a whole other level of awareness of its depths.

The Veil of Time: Layering Histories and Mysteries

The Grand Canyon's past is a big mystery; we cannot wait to explore it. A story lies dormant within every rock layer, crumbling ruin, and cryptic petroglyph.

The canyon is where time seems to fold in on itself, where the past and the present collide in a dance of shadows and light. Unveiling the secrets concealed within its depths requires effort, yet the rewards are immeasurable for those willing to delve deeper.

Echoes of the Past: Unraveling the Enigmatic Landscape

Exploring the Grand Canyon connects you to the ancient people who called this place home. Their presence lingers in the wind, the dancing shadows, and the ancient artifacts and ruins.

The key to unraveling the Grand Canyon's mysteries is to listen to the echoes of the past and decipher the cryptic symbols and messages. Only then can we uncover this mysterious landscape's true nature and secrets.

Guardians of the Canyon: Mythical Beings and Forgotten Spirits

The Grand Canyon is a place of mystery, with mythical creatures and forgotten spirits still haunting the area. The prevailing belief is that the canyon is teeming with powerful spirits, serving as ancient protectors.

Legend has it that these mythical beings hold the key to unlocking the canyon's deepest secrets and can guide you toward enlightenment. However, they are hard to reach, and anyone who wants their wisdom must be ready to face tests and challenges that will measure their bravery and determination.

Secrets Carved in Stone: Hieroglyphs and Messages from the Ancients

One of the most intriguing aspects of the Grand Canyon's mysteries is the countless hieroglyphs and petroglyphs that adorn its walls. The intricate details and weathered surfaces of these ancient carvings tell tales of a civilization long gone. As night descends and the stars twinkle above, the hieroglyphs emanate an otherworldly glow, as if imbued with the spirits of the ancients who once roamed these hallowed grounds. Their voices whisper on the wind, urging the curious seeker to delve deeper, to unravel the secrets carved in stone and unlock the mysteries that lie dormant in the canyon's heart.

Shadows in the Depths: Exploring the Hidden Passages and Caverns

The mystery and intrigue only intensify as one delves further into the Grand Canyon. Within this vast expanse, there are concealed passages and unexplored caves. These subterranean worlds are completely enigmatic, hiding secrets safeguarded by the rocks and dirt.

The Watchers of Time: An Encounter with Timeless Guardians

They say there are ancient guardians in the heart of the Grand Canyon, watching over it for centuries. You hardly see these eternal creatures, but you can feel them in the quiet air and the whispering wind.

According to certain beliefs, the guardians are the ethereal remnants of the canyon's ancient inhabitants, while others perceive them as celestial beings entrusted with its protection. Whether their true nature is known, one thing is undeniable: coming face-to-face with these watchers of time leaves a profound impression.

Lost and Found: Unearthing Artifacts That Defy Explanation

The Grand Canyon has tons of incredible ancient artifacts. Our exhibition features a remarkable collection of artifacts, such as pottery, jewelry, stone tablets, and enigmatic devices. This revelation is astonishing and prompts us to reevaluate our understanding of history.

People who love exploring the canyon found a bunch of these artifacts. However, word on the street is that even bigger treasures await those who dare to go after them.

The Pulse of the Canyon: A Convergence of Mystery and Revelation

As one immerses oneself in the mysteries of the Grand Canyon, one realizes that this place is more than just a natural wonder. It is a nexus of energy and power, where the boundaries between the physical and spiritual realms blur and merge.

There is a pulse that beats within the heart of the canyon, a rhythmic thrum that seems to resonate with the very essence of creation. Those attuned to this pulse speak of visions, revelations, and a deeper understanding of the universe and our place within it.

G.E. Kincaid's Mysterious Expedition

The Cryptic Invitation: A Call to Uncover Hidden Truths

The story of G.E. Kincaid's mysterious expedition to the Grand Canyon begins with a cryptic invitation. In the early 20th century, an adventurer and explorer, Kincaid, received a strange letter from an anonymous source urging him to journey into the canyon's heart.

The letter spoke of ancient secrets and hidden truths of a lost civilization that had once thrived in the canyon's depths. The air crackled with anticipation, signaling an imminent significant event.

Into the Unknown Abyss: The Journey Begins

Intrigued by the mysterious invitation, Kincaid gathered a small team of trusted companions and embarked on a journey into the unknown. Their destination was a remote and rarely explored region of the Grand Canyon, shrouded in mystery and legend.

As they descended into the canyon's depths, the team could feel a sense of anticipation and unease growing with each passing day. The canyon walls closed around them, and strange whispers echoed through the wind as if urging them to turn back.

Whispers of the Ancients: Echoes in the Canyon's Depths

Despite their challenges and obstacles, Kincaid and his team pressed on, driven by a burning desire to uncover the truth. As they ventured deeper into the canyon, they noticed strange markings and symbols carved into the rock walls. These ancient hieroglyphs told a story of a long-forgotten civilization.

The Enigmatic Guide: Following Kincaid's Trail

An unfamiliar figure emerged from the shadows as the mystery surrounding Kincaid's disappearance deepened. Known only as "The Enigmatic Guide," this individual claimed to possess intimate knowledge of Kincaid's expedition and his uncovered secrets. The Guide said they would show anyone brave enough to follow Kincaid's path, revealing the hidden truth.

Intrigued by the Guide's claims, adventurers and researchers set out to retrace Kincaid's journey. Armed with his cryptic notes and maps, they ventured deep into the heart of the Grand Canyon, determined to unravel the enigma that had consumed Kincaid's life.

Veiled in Mystery: Deciphering Cryptic Symbols

As they followed in Kincaid's footsteps, the group encountered the same mysterious petroglyphs and hieroglyphs that had captivated the explorer. The symbols held a cryptic language that defied easy translation. The Enigmatic Guide, however, claimed to possess the key to deciphering their hidden meaning.

Under the Guide's tutelage, the group unraveled the complex web of symbols, revealing a narrative of an ancient civilization with knowledge far beyond their time. The petroglyphs told of advanced technologies, celestial alignments, and a profound understanding of the universe that challenged everything they thought they knew.

Unraveling the Enigma: Secrets Beneath the Surface

As they delved deeper into the canyon's secrets, the group discovered hidden chambers and passages that confirmed Kincaid's theories. The artifacts they unearthed were unlike anything they had ever seen, hinting at a level of sophistication that defied conventional historical narratives.

The Enigmatic Guide urged them, claiming that the ultimate truth lay beyond their reach. Doubts about the Guide's true intentions arose as they ventured deeper into the abyss. Was he leading them toward enlightenment or luring them into a trap?

Echoes of the Past: Revelations That Challenge History

Despite their growing unease, the group pressed on, driven by an insatiable curiosity to uncover the truth. As they pieced together the fragments of the past, a stunning picture emerged. The civilization Kincaid had stumbled upon was not an isolated phenomenon but part of a vast network of ancient cultures that had thrived globally.

The implications were staggering. Kincaid's findings, if proven, would require a complete reevaluation and rewriting of the history of human civilization. Considering this additional evidence, the once widely accepted conventional narratives would crumble.

Into the Abyss: The Expedition's Climactic Revelation

The group faced a decisive moment as they stood on the brink of a revelation that could change the world forever. The Enigmatic Guide revealed he had been withholding the last piece of the puzzle, a profound secret that would shatter their understanding of reality.

But before he could unveil this ultimate truth, chaos erupted. The canyon came alive as if the ancient spirits that dwelled within its depths had awakened to protect their long-held secrets. In the ensuing madness, the Enigmatic Guide vanished, leaving the group to face the consequences of their discovery alone.

Uncovering Ancient Artifacts

The Hidden Chamber Revealed

Deep in the heart of the ancient ruins, a hidden chamber lay shrouded in the aftermath of the Enigmatic Guide's disappearance. The group stood at the threshold of a secret chamber deep within the canyon's heart. The chamber was unlike anything they had ever seen, its walls adorned with intricate carvings and pulsating with otherworldly energy—an encounter with Timeless Relics.

Deep within the hidden chamber, the air was thick with an ancient energy that seemed to pulse through the shadows. As the dim light from our lanterns flickered across the walls, we beheld a sight that filled us with awe and trepidation. Timeless relics adorned the room, each one whispering secrets of civilizations long forgotten.

Golden urns glinted in the dim light, their intricate carvings telling stories of triumph and tragedy. Dust-covered scrolls lay scattered across a stone table, waiting to reveal their enigmatic contents. And in the corner, a gleaming statue stood tall, its features weathered but still radiating a sense of power and mystery.

As we moved closer to examine the relics, a sense of unease settled over us. It was as if the artifacts held a silent vigil, watching our every move with ancient eyes. A chill ran down my spine as I reached out to touch a weathered tablet, its surface smooth beneath my fingers but crackling with a hidden energy.

At that moment, I felt a connection to the past unlike anything I had ever experienced. It was as if the relics were reaching out to us, beckoning us to uncover their hidden truths. As we delved deeper into the chamber, the whispers of lost civilizations grew louder, echoing through the darkness and stirring something primal within our souls.

An Encounter with Timeless Relics

As they stepped into the hidden chamber, the group was immediately struck by the ancient artifacts. The relics were unlike anything they had ever encountered, crafted from materials that defied explanation. Objects emitted an otherworldly glow, while others resonated with a force that evoked a chilling sensation.

Each artifact they stumbled upon in the canyon seemed to carry a hidden message, a key to unlocking the enigmatic mystery that had lured them there. The group worked feverishly to catalog and study the relics, hoping to unravel their secrets.

Whispers of Lost Civilizations

As they delved deeper into studying the artifacts, the group uncovered tantalizing clues about the lost civilization that had created them. The relics spoke of a people who had achieved technological and spiritual advancement that surpassed anything the modern world had ever known.

There were whispers of great cities that had once thrived in the canyon's heart, of flying machines and energy devices that defied the laws of physics. The artifacts whispered tales of a lost civilization, their intricate designs reflecting a profound understanding of the universe.

The Enigmatic Symbols of the Past

The enigmatic symbols adorning the artifacts were central to their mystery. Unlike anything the group had ever seen, these symbols held the key to unlocking the relics' full potential. The group pored over the symbols, trying to decipher their meaning and unlock their secrets.

While engaged in their work, they discovered an intricate knowledge system embedded within the symbols. Like a cosmic code, this language of the universe revealed the enigmatic answers to the age-old questions that had perplexed humanity.

A Mysterious Scroll Unearthed

The group discovered an ancient scroll that was of great significance. With the same mysterious symbols as the other artifacts, the scroll had a distinctive feeling that suggested its long history. The symbols appeared to shimmer slightly, infused with a force beyond their comprehension.

As they carefully unrolled the scroll, they gazed upon a cosmos map. The map was unlike anything they had ever seen, depicting a far vaster and more complex universe than they had ever imagined. At the center of the map was a symbol that pulsed with otherworldly energy, a symbol that held the key to unlocking the ultimate truth.

Intrigue in the Archaeological Dig

As the group's discovery spread, they found themselves at the center of growing intrigue and controversy. Other archaeologists and researchers flocked to the canyon, hoping to uncover the secrets for themselves. Certain individuals aimed to conceal the truth - influential groups viewed the group's revelations as a danger to their own interests.

The group navigated a treacherous landscape of rival factions and hidden agendas, never sure who they could trust. They knew the stakes were higher than ever, and the world's fate might hang in the balance.

Unveiling the Secrets of the Artifacts

As they raced against time to unlock the artifacts' full potential, the group uncovered a series of startling revelations. The relics seemed connected to a grand cosmic cycle, a pattern of creation and destruction that had played out across the ages.

They discovered that the lost civilization had been just one in an extensive line of advanced cultures that had risen and fallen throughout history, each one leaving behind a legacy of knowledge and power. And at the center of it all was a great cosmic force, an energy that tied all of existence together in a vast web of interconnectedness.

Echoes of Ancient Rituals

The group discovered evidence of ancient rituals and ceremonies as they explored the artifacts further. The purpose of these rituals was to tap into the power of the universe through the great cosmic cycle.

The Cryptic Language of the Artifacts

As the group continued to study the artifacts, they realized that the enigmatic symbols adorning them were more than mere decorations. They were, in fact, a complex language that held the key to unlocking the true power of the relics. The symbols seemed alive, pulsating with an energy that drew the researchers deeper into their mysteries.

The group worked tirelessly to decipher the cryptic language, poring over ancient texts and consulting with experts in the field. Slowly but surely, they unraveled the secrets of the symbols, piecing together a narrative that spoke of an ancient civilization with knowledge and abilities far beyond anything they had ever encountered.

Confronting the Mysteries of the Past

As the true nature of the artifacts revealed itself, the group found themselves confronted with a series of profound questions. How had this ancient civilization achieved such a level of advancement? What led to the loss of their knowledge and their fate?

The answers seemed to lie in the very fabric of the universe, a cosmos far more complex and interconnected than they had ever imagined. The artifacts were not just relics of a bygone age, but a testament to a more profound truth about reality itself.

Shadows of a Cover-Up

While the group found the discoveries fascinating, they also had a feeling of being under scrutiny. Shadowy figures lurked in the background; powerful interests that seemed determined to keep the truth hidden from the world.

As they dug deeper, they uncovered evidence of a vast conspiracy stretching back centuries, a web of deceit and manipulation designed to keep the secrets of the past buried forever. The group realized they were not just racing against time, but against forces that would stop at nothing to maintain the status quo.

Unraveling the Web of Deception

Determined to expose the truth, the group pressed on, following a trail of clues that led them deeper into the heart of the conspiracy. They uncovered secret societies and agendas, influential figures manipulating history for their gain.

But even as they unraveled the web of deception, they realized that the true nature of the conspiracy was more complex and far-reaching than they had ever imagined. The knowledge they had gained was just a small glimpse of a greater problem, and the potential repercussions of what lay beneath were immense.

Illuminating the Dark Corner of Deception

In the end, the artifacts themselves provided the key to unlocking the ultimate piece of the puzzle. As the group delved deeper into their secrets, they discovered a hidden message encoded into the very fabric of the relics.

The message spoke of a tremendous cosmic cycle, a pattern of creation and destruction that had played out across the ages. It revealed that the ancient civilization had been just one in an extensive line of advanced cultures that had risen and fallen throughout history, each one leaving behind a legacy of knowledge and power.

But the message also contained a warning, a dire prophecy of a future ahead. It spoke of a great cataclysm that would soon engulf the world, a time of chaos and upheaval that would evaluate the very limits of human resilience.

Part II: The Depths of Conspiracy

Delving into the Unknown: A Cloak of Mystery Surrounding Ancient Discoveries

As the group grappled with the implications of their discoveries, they found themselves drawn deeper into a world of mystery and intrigue. The uncovered artifacts were just the start, providing a captivating glimpse into a forgotten history.

But even as they marveled at the wonders they had found; they could feel the weight of the unknown pressing down upon them. There were too many questions left unanswered and too many secrets that remained hidden in the shadows.

Whispers of Intrigue: Uncovering Hidden Agenda and Secret Motivations

While investigating, the group revealed a complex system of hidden agendas and undisclosed motivations that influenced all aspects of their work. Influential forces and individuals deliberately suppressed the truth.

The more they dug, the more they realized that the conspiracy they had stumbled upon was far more complex than they had ever imagined. There were layers of deception, each more intricate than the last.

Dark Shadows: The Enigmatic Figures Behind the Veil of Secrecy

The conspiracy revolved around a shadowy group of enigmatic individuals who were the puppet experts, pulling the strings behind the scenes.

The group worked tirelessly to uncover their identities, but every lead they followed seemed to lead to a dead end. The figures behind the veil of secrecy were like ghosts, elusive and always one step ahead.

Trails of Deception: Unraveling the Twisted Paths of Manipulation and Betrayal

As the group delved deeper into the conspiracy, they navigated a treacherous landscape of manipulation and betrayal. They uncovered evidence of secret societies and ancient orders, each with its agenda and motivations.

They realized that the truth they sought was not just uncovering ancient artifacts and deciphering cryptic messages. They had to untangle the web of deceit and distinguish between truth and lies.

Cryptic Messages: Decrypting Clues and Codes That Lead to the Truth

Despite facing challenges, the group refused to give up. They believed that truth lived in an undiscovered location, awaiting revelation. So, they continued to follow a trail of cryptic messages and hidden clues that led them closer to the heart of the mystery.

With furrowed brows, they delved into
the depths of ancient texts, deciphering
intricate ciphers, and connecting the
fragments of a puzzle that had spanned
centuries. Piece by piece, they
painstakingly revealed the deeply
entrenched secrets that had remained
hidden for countless generations.

Layers of Deceit: Peeling Back the Facade to Reveal the Core of Conspiracy

But even as they made progress, they realized that the conspiracy they had uncovered was far more insidious than they had ever imagined. The layers of deceit seemed to go on forever, each revealing a new level of manipulation and control.

They discovered that the ancient artifacts they had found were just a tiny part of a much larger mystery. The true nature of the conspiracy was far more profound, threatening to shake the foundations of everything they thought they knew.

Echoes of the Past: Ancient Echoes Resonating Through Time with Sinister Purpose

As they delved deeper into the heart of the mystery, the group uncovered evidence of an ancient evil lurking in the shadows for centuries. They discovered that the artifacts they had uncovered were relics of a bygone age and tools of power wielded by those who sought to control the course of history.

They realized that the echoes of the past were not just echoes but a sinister force resonating through time, shaping the course of human events in ways that were too terrible to contemplate.

Forbidden Knowledge: The Price of Seeking Truth in a World Shrouded in Lies

As the true nature of the conspiracy revealed itself, the group grappled with the consequences of their actions. They had set out to uncover the truth, but now they realized that the price of that truth might be higher than they had ever imagined.

They had stumbled upon a world of forbidden knowledge, a realm where the very fabric of reality seemed to unravel. After uncovering the secrets, they understood they were forever bound by the haunting knowledge and could not retreat.

Unmasking the Puppeteers: Exposing the Masterminds Pulling Strings from the Shadows

As the group delved deeper into the heart of the conspiracy, they pieced together the identities of the enigmatic figures pulling the strings from behind the scenes. They uncovered a network of influential individuals and organizations manipulating history for centuries.

At the center of this web was a shadowy cabal known only as the Puppeteers, a group of ancient entities that had been guiding human events since the dawn of civilization. The group realized that the artifacts they had uncovered were just one small part of a much larger plan, a grand design set in motion long before they were born.

The Veil Lifts: Illuminating the Dark Secret and Unveiling the Sinister Truth

As the last pieces of the puzzle fell into place, the group stood on the precipice of a revelation that threatened to shake the very foundations of their understanding. They had uncovered a truth so profound and terrifying that it defied all logic and reason.

They realized that the ancient civilization they had been studying was not just a forgotten relic of the past but a warning of a future yet to come. The unearthed artifacts held significance beyond their utilitarian purpose; they prophesied a forthcoming cataclysm that would engulf the world.

The Veil of Secrecy

A Dark History Uncovered

As the group processed their findings, they realized they had unearthed a long-forgotten history, shrouded in secrecy. The ancient civilization they were studying was not nice, but a society based on manipulation, control, and exploitation.

They found evidence of messed-up stuff that happened in the name of progress, like wiping out entire populations for power. They realized that this ancient civilization's legacy was one of darkness and despair, a warning of the dangers of unchecked ambition.

Whispers in the Shadow

Even as they struggled to accept the weight of their discovery, the group sensed they were not alone in their pursuit of the truth. They caught glimpses of shadowy figures lurking in the darkness and heard whispers of secret organizations that had been working to conceal the truth for generations.

They realized they had stumbled into a world of secrets and lies, a realm where nothing was as it seemed. They knew they would have to tread carefully if they were to survive the dangers ahead.

The Elusive Trail of Clues

Despite the challenges they faced, the group remained stubborn. They knew the truth was out there, like a hidden treasure, and they were determined to find the breadcrumbs of evidence. They carefully looked at old manuscripts and figured out mysterious notes, putting together a puzzle from the past. As they followed the winding path, the air grew heavy with the weight of secrets and lies, a constant reminder of the truth they were determined to unveil.

Cloaked in Mystery

As they delved deeper into the heart of the mystery, the group realized they had entered a world cloaked in shadows and secrets. They encountered enigmatic figures who spoke riddles and cryptic messages, each one leading them closer to the truth even as it seemed to slip further out of reach.

They realized that the veil of secrecy draped over the ancient civilization was not just a means of concealment, but a powerful tool of control. Those who held the secrets held the power, and they would stop at nothing to keep their grip on that power.

Agents of Disinformation

As the group continued their investigation, they encountered resistance from unexpected quarters. They realized that powerful forces at work, individuals, and organizations were determined to keep the truth buried at all costs.

They encountered agents of disinformation, shadowy figures who worked to spread lies and confusion, sowing doubt, and discord among those who sought the truth. They realized they were up against an enemy who was both ruthless and cunning, one who would stop at nothing to maintain the status quo.

Unraveling the Threads of Deceit

Despite the challenges they faced, the group refused to give up. Driven by the anticipation of unraveling a mysterious truth, they remained determined to follow the convoluted trails of deceit wherever they may lead.

As they delved deeper into the web of lies and manipulation, they uncovered a labyrinth of secrets, each thread leading to another layer of deceit. They uncovered secret societies and ancient orders, each with their agenda and motivations, each playing a role in the grand design that had been set in motion so long ago.

Secrets Within Secrets

As they peeled back the layers of deception, the group realized that their uncovered secrets were just the beginning. They discovered secrets within secrets, a labyrinth of hidden truths that seemed to stretch on into infinity.

They encountered cryptic symbols and enigmatic messages, each leading them deeper into the heart of the mystery. They realized that the ancient civilization they had been studying was not just a relic of the past but a living entity that had never indeed died.

Forbidden Knowledge Revealed

The group studied the relics they found and noticed patterns and connections hiding right before them. As they examined the artifacts, a sense of secrecy and mystery lingered, hinting at forbidden knowledge from a distant past. These secrets had remained concealed for centuries and could change the course of history.

The Cryptic Language of Power

As they delved deeper into the secrets of the artifacts, the group realized they were dealing with a language of power that transcended mere words. The symbols and glyphs that adorned the relics were not just decorative flourishes, but a complex system of communication used by ancient civilizations to encode their most sacred truths.

When they deciphered the mysterious language, they became able to unlock the artifact's true potential. They knew that if they could decipher this language, they would hold the key to a power that could change the world.

Breaking Through the Veil

The group could only uncover the truth by breaking through the veil of secrecy. They confronted the dark forces, shining a light on the shadows and revealing hidden lies.

They realized the price of truth was high, and their path was fraught with danger and uncertainty. But they also knew the alternative was a world of darkness and despair, a future too terrible to contemplate.

Hidden Artifacts, Hidden Truths

The Cryptic Cave: A Discovery Beyond Imagination

As the group followed the trail of clues left behind by the ancient civilization, they stood at the entrance to a cave that defied all logic and reason. The entrance hid in plain sight, a subtle irregularity in the rock face that the untrained eye could easily overlook.

But as they stepped inside, they realized they had stumbled upon a discovery beyond anything they could have ever imagined. The cave was vast and sprawling, a labyrinth of twisting passages and hidden chambers stretching into infinity.

Echoes of Ancient Civilizations: Traces in the Shadows

As they explored the depths of the cryptic cave, the group uncovered traces of the ancient civilization that had once called this place home. They discovered intricate carvings and enigmatic symbols etched into the walls, each telling a story of a people who had achieved an almost unimaginable level of knowledge and power.

They realized the cave was not just a physical space, but a repository of ancient wisdom hidden from the world for centuries. They knew that if they could decipher the secrets within, they would hold the key to unlocking a power that could change the course of human history.

Echoes of Ancient Civilizations: Traces in the Shadows

Cryptic cave shadows echo with ancient whispers, uncovering traces of forgotten civilizations. Lingering in the air are traces of a bygone era, teasing with hidden secrets and revelations. As the dim light dances across the walls, intricate patterns and symbols come to life, leaving a trail of enigmatic stories etched in stone.

The walls witness the passing of time, capturing moments frozen in history. Symbols of unknown origin decorate the chamber, telling tales of forgotten rituals and ancient rites. Ancient symbols and images entwine, creating a rich tapestry of secrets, beckoning only the courageous to unveil the hidden truths lurking in the shadows.

Amidst the fading echoes of ancient voices, a long-lost civilization hangs heavy in the air. The cave becomes a portal to a realm shrouded in mystery, where the boundary between reality and legend blurs. Whispers of a forgotten past beckon the curious traveler deeper into the shadows, promising revelations that defy explanation.

The air gets all tense, like the walls are hiding secrets. Moving forward is like embarking on a journey into the unknown, discovering the echoes of lost civilizations with a captivating allure. The enigmatic cave pays homage to our ancestors, with their untold tales awaiting discovery by intrepid adventurers who dare to uncover ancient mysteries.

The Forbidden Relics: Whispers of the Past

As the group delved deeper into the cryptic cave, they uncovered several artifacts that defy all explanations. These relics were unlike anything they had ever seen, crafted from materials that seemed to shimmer and glow with an otherworldly light.

They realized these artifacts were not mere trinkets or decorative objects, but powerful tools imbued with an almost unimaginable level of knowledge and power. They could feel the energy emanating from the relics, a pulsing, throbbing force that seemed to reach out and touch their souls.

Enigmatic Symbols: Keys to Unlocking Mysteries

The group studied the artifacts more closely and noticed enigmatic symbols etched into their surfaces. These symbols were unlike anything they had ever seen, a cryptic language that held the key to unlocking the mysteries of ancient civilization.

They realized these symbols were not just mere decorations, but a complex communication system used by the ancients to encode their most sacred truths. They knew that if they could decipher the meaning behind these symbols, they would hold the key to a power that could change the world.

The Enchanted Artefacts: Powers Unveiled

As they continued to explore the depths of the cryptic cave, the group uncovered increased artifacts that possessed a strange and otherworldly power. They discovered ancient scrolls and tomes glowed with ethereal light, weapons, and tools that thrummed with a pulsing, vibrant energy.

They came to understand that these artifacts were not ordinary items, but vessels of a concealed power dating back centuries. They knew that if they could harness this power, they would hold the key to unlocking an almost unimaginable level of knowledge and understanding.

Guardians of the Secrets: Keepers of the Truth

But as they delved deeper into the mysteries of the cryptic cave, the group sensed they were not alone. An unseen force protected the secrets of ancient civilization.

They realized that this presence was not nasty, but a guardian tasked with protecting the knowledge and power within the cave. Recognizing that trust was key, they understood that gaining the guardian's confidence would reveal a truth kept hidden from the world for centuries.

Unearthed Treasures: Revealing Lost Histories

As they continued to explore the depths of the cryptic cave, the group uncovered more treasures that held the key to unlocking the secrets of the ancient civilization. They discovered ancient maps and charts that depicted a world vastly different from the one they knew, a world filled with wonder and mystery.

They realized these treasures were mere artifacts and a window into a lost history that the world had forgotten. They knew that if they could piece together the fragments of this history, they would hold the key to unlocking a truth that could change the course of human civilization.

The Pulse of the Canyon: A Convergence of Mystery and Revelation

As they emerged from the depths of the cryptic cave, the group realized that the experience had forever changed them. They had witnessed things that defied all explanation and encountered truths that challenged everything they thought they knew about the world.

They realized that the canyon itself was a living entity, a place where the boundaries between the physical and spiritual realms had blurred. They could feel the pulse of the canyon thrumming through their veins, a powerful force that guided them toward a destiny beyond their wildest imaginings.

Unraveling the Web of Deception

The Looming Shadows of Secrecy

But even as they basked in their newfound knowledge, the group sensed they were not alone in pursuing the truth. They could feel the looming shadows of secrecy closing in around them, darkness threatening to engulf everything they had worked so hard to uncover.

Whisperings of Betrayal and Conspiracy

As they delved deeper into the web of deception surrounding the ancient civilization, the group heard whispers of betrayal and conspiracy that seemed to emanate from every corner of the canyon. They realized they were not the first ones to stumble upon the secrets of the cryptic cave and that powerful forces were at work that would stop at nothing to keep the truth hidden from the world.

They stumbled upon eerie figures lurking in the shadows, whose intentions appeared sinister and incomprehensible. They realized they were up against an enemy that was both cunning and ruthless and would not hesitate to use any means necessary to achieve their goals.

Threads of Deception Woven Within History

As they continued to unravel the threads of deception woven throughout history, the group realized that the conspiracy they had uncovered was far vaster and more complex than they had ever imagined. They discovered that the ancient civilization they studied was just one small piece of a much larger puzzle, a grand design set in motion centuries ago.

They realized the artifacts they had uncovered were not just mere trinkets or relics but powerful tools to shape human history. They knew that if they could decipher the secrets within these artifacts, they would hold the key to unlocking a truth that could change the world forever.

Tangled Lies and Half-Truths

But as they delved deeper into the heart of the conspiracy, the group encountered a web of lies and half-truths that seemed designed to lead them astray. They discovered they were facing a foe who was not just clever and merciless, but also remarkably skilled at deceiving others.

They encountered false leads and dead ends, trails that seemed to go nowhere, and clues that only led them deeper into the labyrinth of confusion. They knew that they would have to be incredibly careful if they hoped to unravel the tangled web of lies woven around them.

Intricate Patterns of Manipulation

Through their ongoing study of the artifacts and clues, they made continuous discoveries. They realized that the ancient civilization they had been studying was not just a relic of the past but a powerful force shaping the course of human events for centuries.

The artifacts they found were more than just tools; they held a hidden power unknown for generations. They knew that if they could harness this power, they would hold the key to unlocking an almost unimaginable level of knowledge and understanding.

The Elusive Key to Unlocking the Truth

But even as they drew closer to the heart of the mystery, the group realized that the key to unlocking the truth was still eluding them. Despite their efforts in uncovering clues and artifacts, they could not escape the feeling that there was still an elusive part of the puzzle.

They knew they would have to keep searching and digging deeper into the heart of the conspiracy if they hoped to uncover the truth. They acknowledged the perilous road ahead, yet were determined to press on, knowing they were nearing the long-awaited answers.

Unraveling the Cryptic Code of Deception

In the end, the cryptic code of deception held the key to unlocking the truth. As they studied the intricate patterns of manipulation and deceit woven throughout history, the group noticed a pattern emerging, a code that seemed to hide in plain sight.

They realized that the artifacts they had uncovered were not mere tools, but a language of power that the ancient civilization had used to communicate their most sacred truths. They knew that if they could decipher this language, they would hold the key to unlocking an almost unimaginable knowledge and understanding.

Layers of Deceit Revealed

As they continued to unravel the cryptic code of deception, the group began peeling back the layers of deceit woven around the ancient civilization. The conspiracy they discovered went beyond mere secrecy and manipulation.

They discovered that the artifacts they had uncovered were not just tools, but powerful weapons used to shape human history. They realized that the ancient civilization had been a passive observer of human events and an active participant in shaping the world's destiny.

The Unraveled Threads of a Sinister Plot

While exploring the conspiracy further, the team discovered a dark scheme that had remained unnoticed for centuries. They realized that the ancient civilization had not just been a benevolent force for good but a powerful entity that had been manipulating the course of human events for its own sinister purposes.

They discovered that the artifacts they had uncovered were not mere tools but a means to an end, a way for the ancient civilization to exert its influence over the world. They knew that if they could expose this plot, they would hold the key to unlocking a truth that could change the course of human history forever.

Illuminating the Dark Corner of Deception

In the end, only by illuminating the dark corners of deception could the group uncover the truth. They had to confront the lies and half-truths woven around them to shine a light into the shadows and expose the sinister forces that had been manipulating the world for centuries.

They realized that the price of truth was high and that their path was fraught with danger and uncertainty. But they also knew the alternative was a world of darkness and despair, a future too terrible to contemplate.

Part III: Cultural and Historical Implications

The Whispers of Ancient Civilizations

As the group emerged from the depths of the conspiracy, they realized that the implications of their discovery were far-reaching and profound. They had uncovered a truth that challenged everything they thought they knew about the world, a truth that had the power to reshape the course of human history.

They realized that the ancient civilization they had been studying was not just a relic of the past but a powerful force that had been shaping the course of human events for centuries. They knew that if they could decipher the secrets that lay within the artifacts they had uncovered, they would hold the key to unlocking an almost unimaginable level of knowledge and understanding.

Echoes of a Forgotten Past

While examining the unearthed artifacts and evidence, the group heard reverberations of a forgotten past echoing through the ages. They realized that the ancient civilization they had been studying was not just a single entity, but a complex tapestry of cultures and traditions woven together over centuries.

They discovered that the artifacts they had uncovered were not just mere tools, but a testament to the ingenuity and creativity of ancient civilization. They knew that if they could unravel the mysteries within these artifacts, they would hold the key to unlocking a lost history that the world had forgotten.

The Enigmatic Artefact That Defies Explanation

But even as they continued to uncover more pieces of the puzzle, the group realized that there was one artifact that defied all explanations. It was a small, unassuming object that seemed to pulse with a strange, otherworldly energy, an energy that seemed to reach out and touch their very souls.

They realized this artifact was not just a mere trinket or relic, but a powerful conduit of a force beyond their understanding. They knew that if they could decipher the secrets within this artifact, they would hold the key to unlocking a truth that could change the course of human history forever.

Lost Knowledge and Hidden Wisdom

While exploring the enigmatic artifact further, the group discovered a treasure trove of ancient knowledge and hidden wisdom that had remained concealed for centuries. They realized that the ancient civilization they had been studying was not just a primitive society but a highly advanced culture that had achieved an almost unimaginable level of understanding and sophistication.

They discovered that the artifact they had uncovered was a mere trinket or relic and a repository of ancient knowledge carefully preserved and passed down through the generations. They knew that if they could decipher the secrets within this artifact, they would hold the key to unlocking a truth that could change the world forever.

Unraveling the Threads of Time

While exploring the intricate history of ancient civilization, the group realized the profound implications of their discovery exceeded their wildest imagination. The artifacts they found were more than tools; they were a testament to the enduring power of the human spirit.

They discovered ancient civilizations had been passive observers of the world and active participants in shaping the course of human history. They knew that if they could decipher the secrets within these artifacts, they would hold the key to unlocking a truth that could change how we understand ourselves and our place in the universe.

The Cryptic Symbols That Speak Volumes

As the group delved further into studying the artifacts and clues, they stumbled upon a set of cryptic symbols intricately intertwined within the tapestry of an ancient civilization. More than ornamental, these symbols were a powerful way to communicate deep universal truths.

They discovered that the symbols they had uncovered were mere markings or glyphs and a testament to the ancient civilization's profound spiritual and philosophical beliefs. They knew that if they could decipher the meaning behind these symbols, they would hold the key to unlocking a truth that could change how we understand the nature of reality.

The Astonishing Discoveries That Challenge Conventional Wisdom

As they continued to uncover more pieces of the puzzle, the group realized their discoveries were genuinely astonishing. They had uncovered a truth that challenged everything they thought they knew about the world, a truth that had the power to reshape the course of human history.

They realized that the ancient civilization they had been studying was not just a primitive society but a highly advanced culture that had achieved an almost unimaginable level of understanding and sophistication. They knew that if they could share their discoveries with the world, they would hold the key to unlocking a new era of enlightenment and understanding.

The Puzzle Pieces of History Fit Together

As they stepped back and looked at the bigger picture, the group realized that the pieces of the puzzle they had been working on for so long were finally fitting together. They realized that the ancient civilization they had been studying was not just an isolated phenomenon, but a crucial piece of a much larger tapestry woven throughout the ages.

The artifacts they had uncovered turned out to be more than mere tools; they were a testament to the enduring power of the human spirit. They knew that if they could share their discoveries with the world, they would hold the key to unlocking a new era of understanding and enlightenment that could change the course of human history forever.

Portals to Another Era: Mysteries of the Kincaid Expedition

Through their ongoing exploration of the ancient civilization's mysteries, the team realized that the Kincaid Expedition was not a minor historical detail, but a crucial piece of the puzzle that had been right in front of them all along. Kincaid's discoveries were not trivial; they opened the doors to a forgotten world lost in the depths of time.

The Legacy of Secrets That Could Shake the Foundations of Our Understanding

The more the group investigated the Kincaid Expedition, the more they understood that the secrets they uncovered could profoundly affect our perception of the world. Kincaid's findings were more than just artifacts; they were a testament to the enduring strength of humanity.

They discovered that the ancient civilization that Kincaid had stumbled upon was not just a primitive society but a highly advanced culture that had achieved a level of understanding and almost unimaginable sophistication. They knew that if they could share Kincaid's discoveries with the world, they would hold the key to unlocking a new era of enlightenment and understanding.

The Secrets That Could Rewrite History

The Hidden Chambers of the Past

As they kept exploring the past's hidden chambers, the group found additional centuries-old secrets. They realized that the ancient civilization they had been studying was more than just a curiosity; it was a vital part of a hidden puzzle.

The chambers they unveiled were not mere rooms, but a testament to the ancient civilization's ingenuity and creativity. The secrets within these chambers, if deciphered, could rewrite our understanding of the world's fabric, a discovery of immense significance and excitement.

Whispers of Ancient Civilizations

As they continued to explore the hidden chambers of the past, the group heard whispers of ancient civilizations that seemed to echo throughout the ages. Realizing the broader context, they understood that the civilization they had been studying was not an isolated phenomenon but a piece of a much larger tapestry of interconnected cultures and traditions that had developed over centuries.

The whispers they had heard turned out to be more than mere legends or myths; they were a testament to the enduring power of the human spirit. Recognizing that deciphering the enigmatic murmurs held the power to unveil a concealed narrative, they understood they would possess the means to transform our perception of ourselves and our role in the universe.

The Enigmatic Artefacts That Defy Explanation

As they continued to uncover more artifacts from the ancient civilization, the group realized that some of these objects seemed to defy all explanation. They were unlike anything they had ever seen, crafted with a level of skill and precision that seemed almost impossible for a civilization of that era.

They realized these artifacts were not just mere trinkets or relics but a testament to the advanced technology and sophisticated understanding of ancient civilization. Recognizing that the secrets harbored by these artifacts held immense significance, they understood that deciphering them could unlock a lost history capable of permanently reshaping the trajectory of human civilization.

Cryptic Inscriptions and Lost Languages

As they delved deeper into the artifacts, the group discerned a series of cryptic inscriptions and lost languages interwoven throughout ancient civilization. They understood these inscriptions were more than just symbols; they were a profound language used to communicate the universe's deepest truths.

The unearthed inscriptions turned out to be more than just decorations, shedding light on the ancient civilization's profound spiritual and philosophical beliefs. They knew that if they could decipher the meaning behind these inscriptions, they would hold the key to unlocking a lost wisdom that could change how we understand the nature of reality.

Unraveling the Mysteries of Time

As they continued to unravel the mysteries of ancient civilization, the group realized that the implications of their discovery were far more profound than they had ever imagined. The civilization they had been studying turned out to be more than just a footnote in history - it was a crucial piece of a much larger puzzle that had remained hidden for generations. They discovered that the mysteries they had uncovered were not just mere curiosities, but a testament to the enduring power of time. They knew that if they could decipher the secrets within these mysteries, they would hold the key to unlocking a lost history that could change how we understand the very nature of existence.

Clues from the Shadows of Antiquity

As they continued to explore the hidden chambers of the past, the group uncovered increasing clues that seemed to emerge from the very shadows of antiquity itself. They understood these clues were not coincidental but carefully crafted hints left by an ancient civilization.

The clues they had uncovered were not just mere hints or suggestions; instead, they were a powerful testament to the ingenuity and foresight of ancient civilization. They knew that if they could follow this trail of clues to its conclusion, they would hold the key to unlocking a lost history that could change the course of human destiny itself.

The Conspiracies that Shroud Historical Truths

As they continued to unravel the mysteries of the ancient civilization, the group realized that there were powerful forces at work that seemed determined to keep the truth hidden from view. They realized that the conspiracies they had uncovered were not just mere theories or speculation, but a deliberate attempt to obscure the true nature of the ancient civilization.

They discovered that the conspiracies they had uncovered were not just mere coincidences or happenstance, but a powerful testament to the enduring power of secrecy. They knew that if they could expose these conspiracies and bring the truth to light, they would hold the key to unlocking a lost history that could change how we understand the very nature of power itself.

Echoes of a Forgotten Era

As we ventured deeper into the hidden chambers of the past, the echoes of a forgotten era reverberated. These echoes were not mere whispers or murmurs, but a powerful testament to the enduring legacy of the ancient civilization.

The echoes we discovered were more than just reverberations; they were a living testament to ancient civilization. This realization fueled our determination to decipher the meaning behind these echoes, as we knew it could unlock a lost wisdom that could change the way we understand the very essence of what it means to be human.

Unveiling the Untold Secrets of the Ancients

As they stood on the brink of a discovery that could change the course of human history forever, the group realized that the secrets they had uncovered were not mere facts or figures, but a powerful testament to the enduring mystery of ancient civilization. Unveiling these secrets and bringing them to light would give them the key to unlocking a lost history that could reshape our understanding of reality.

The secrets they had uncovered were more than curiosities or oddities; they were a powerful testament to the enduring power of the human spirit. With the ability to share these secrets with the world, they understood they would hold the key to unlocking a new era of enlightenment and understanding that might reshape human destiny.

The Revelations That Could Alter Our Perception of History

As they stood on the precipice of a discovery that could shake the very foundations of our understanding of the world, the group realized that the revelations they had uncovered were not just mere facts or figures, but a powerful testament to the enduring mystery of the universe itself. They knew that if they could bring these revelations to light, they would hold the key to unlocking a lost history that could change the way we perceive the very nature of reality itself.

They discovered that the revelations they had uncovered were not just mere curiosities or oddities, but a powerful testament to the enduring power of truth itself. They knew that if they could share these revelations with the world, they would hold the key to unlocking a new era of enlightenment and understanding that could change the course of human history forever.

Challenging Narratives and Timeless Discoveries

The Whispering Winds of the Past

As the group stood amidst the ancient ruins, the whispering winds of the past seemed to carry with them the echoes of a long-forgotten era. The atmosphere was heavy with the burden of the past, and every inhalation felt infused with the spirit of the long-gone civilization that once flourished here.

They realized that the whispers they heard were not just mere figments of their imagination, but a powerful testament to the enduring legacy of the past. They knew that if they could decipher the meaning behind these whispers, they would hold the key to unlocking a lost history that could change how we understand the very nature of time.

Shadows in the Archives: Unveiling Untold Histories

As they delved deeper into the archives of the past, the group uncovered more shadows that obscured the true nature of the ancient civilization. They realized these shadows were not just mere absences of light but a deliberate attempt to hide the untold histories of the past.

The archives they discovered contained both knowledge and a testament to the lasting influence of secrets. They knew that if they could unveil these untold histories and bring them to light, they would hold the key to unlocking a lost wisdom that could change the way we understand the very essence of what it means to be human.

Echoes of Forgotten Tales: Uncovering Lost Civilizations

As they continued to explore the hidden chambers of the past, the group heard echoes of forgotten tales that seemed to resonate throughout the ages. They realized these tales held more significance than mere stories, proving that lost civilizations still have relevance.

They discovered that the stories they had found were more than just tales - they were a real testament to ancient civilization. Decoding the essence of these narratives would grant them the power to unlock a forgotten history, altering our comprehension of existence.

The Enigma of Ancient Symbols: Decoding Mystery Scripts

As they studied the uncovered artifacts, the group noticed a series of ancient symbols and mystery scripts that seemed woven throughout the ancient civilization's tapestry. They understood these symbols held more than simple markings or inscriptions; they were a potent language conveying the most profound truths of the cosmos.

The realization dawned upon them that the symbols they had uncovered were significant curios or peculiarities, but a potent testament to the profound understanding and sophisticated beliefs of the ancient civilization. They knew that if they could decode the meaning behind these symbols, they would hold the key to unlocking lost wisdom that could change how we understand the very nature of existence.

Mythical Beings and Divine Creatures: Legends That Shape Reality

As they continued to unravel the mysteries of ancient civilization, the group encountered stories of mythical beings and divine creatures woven throughout the fabric of the ancient culture. They realized these stories were not mere fantasies or imaginations, but powerful testaments to the enduring power of legends and myths.

The legends they unearthed were not mere tales, but tangible testaments to an ancient civilization. They knew that if they could understand the true nature of these legends, they would hold the key to unlocking a lost wisdom that could change the way we know the very essence of what it means to be human.

Portals to Another Time: Exploring Temporal Anomalies

As they delved deeper into the mysteries of ancient civilization, the group noticed strange temporal anomalies and portals that defied the very laws of physics. As they delved deeper into their research, they comprehended these anomalies were far more than just glitches or aberrations; they were a striking testament to the ancient civilization's unparalleled wisdom and sophisticated technological achievements.

They discovered that the portals they had uncovered were not mere gateways or passages but living testaments to the enduring power of time. They knew that if they could explore these temporal anomalies and unravel their secrets, they would hold the key to unlocking a lost history that could change how we understand the very fabric of reality.

The Quest for Truth: Confronting Established Narratives

As they stood on the brink of a discovery that could challenge the foundations of established history, the group realized that their quest for truth was not just a mere academic pursuit, but a powerful testament to the enduring power of the human spirit. They knew that if they could confront these established narratives and bring the truth to light, they would hold the key to unlocking a new era of enlightenment and understanding.

What they discovered was not just a mere collection of facts or figures, but a living testament to the enduring power of knowledge itself. They knew that if they could share this truth with the world, they would hold the key to unlocking a new era of wisdom and understanding that could change the course of human history forever.

Relics of a Bygone Era: Artifacts That Defy Explanation

As they explored the hidden chambers of the past, the group uncovered more relics and artifacts that defied all explanations. They realized these artifacts were not mere objects or curiosities, but powerful testaments to the enduring mystery of ancient civilization.

Uncovering the relics, they discovered that these were not mere treasures or valuables, but a living testament to the spirit of the ancient civilization. The secrets concealed within these artifacts held the potential to unveil a lost history that could alter our perception of what it truly means to be human.

From Legend to Legacy: Stories That Stand the Test of Time

As they stood amidst the ancient ruins, the group realized that the stories they had uncovered were not mere legends or myths, but a powerful testament to the enduring legacy of ancient civilization. They knew that if they could bring these stories to light and share them with the world, they would hold the key to unlocking a new era of understanding and appreciation for the wisdom of the past.

As they delved deeper into their findings, they realized that the legacy they had stumbled upon was not a simple compilation of stories, but a powerful testament to the resilience of humanity. They knew that if they could preserve this legacy and pass it down to future generations, they would hold the key to unlocking a new era of enlightenment and understanding that could change the course of human history forever.

Illuminating the Darkness: Seeking Enlightenment in the Shadows

As they stood on the precipice of a discovery that could change the world, the group realized their journey was not just a mere quest for knowledge, but a powerful testament to the enduring power of the human spirit. Recognizing that enlightenment lies within the shadows, they understood that unlocking a new era of wisdom and understanding was possible.

They discovered that the enlightenment they had sought was not just a mere state of mind or being, but a living testament to the enduring power of the soul itself. Holding the key to unlocking a new era of peace and harmony that could change the course of human destiny forever, they knew that if they could embrace this enlightenment and share it with the world.

The Power of Myth and the Mysteries of the Past

Opening the Gates of Time

Stepping through the portal, the group discovered a realm that existed beyond the boundaries of time and space. The air was dense with the historical legacy, and every breath they inhaled seemed to contain the essence of the ancient civilization that had once prospered in this exact location.

They realized that the gates they had opened were not just mere doorways or thresholds, but a powerful testament to the enduring mystery of time itself. They knew that if they could unravel the secrets behind these gates, they would hold the key to unlocking a lost history that could change the way we understand the very fabric of reality itself.

Ancient Legends Unveiled

Ancient Legends Unveiled

During their exploration of the timeless realm, the group stumbled upon ancient legends and myths that had remained hidden for centuries. These stories spoke of powerful gods and goddesses, of epic battles and heroic quests, and of a civilization that had achieved a level of wisdom and understanding far beyond anything the modern world had ever known.

They realized these legends were not just mere stories or tales, but a powerful testament to the enduring legacy of the ancient civilization. They knew that if they could unveil these legends and bring them to light, they would hold the key to unlocking a new era of understanding and appreciation for the wisdom of the past.

Echoes of Forgotten Empires

As they delved deeper into the mysteries of the past, the group heard echoes of forgotten empires and lost civilizations. These echoes spoke of a time when the world was a vastly different place, when great cities rose and fell, and when the boundaries between the mortal and the divine were far more fluid than they are today.

They realized these echoes were not just mere reverberations or reflections, but a powerful testament to the enduring power of history itself. They knew that if they could decipher the meaning behind these echoes, they would hold the key to unlocking a lost wisdom that could change the way we understand the very essence of what it means to be human.

Symbols That Speak Across Millennia

As they studied the artifacts and relics they had uncovered, the group noticed a series of symbols and glyphs that seemed to speak across millennia. These symbols were unlike anything they had ever seen, yet they held a power and meaning that transcended time and space.

They realized these symbols were not simple markings or inscriptions, but a profound language that conveyed the deepest truths of the universe. They knew that if they could decode the meaning behind these symbols, they would hold the key to unlocking lost wisdom that could change how we understand the very nature of existence.

The Enigmatic Connection Between Myth and Reality

As they continued to explore the timeless realm, the group noticed a strange and enigmatic connection between the myths and legends they had uncovered and the reality they had left behind. The connection between the two worlds was undeniable, with the past offering a treasure trove of solutions to present-day puzzles.

They understood that this connection went beyond coincidence or fate, proving the enduring power of myth. They knew that if they could unravel the secrets behind this connection, they would hold the key to unlocking a new era of understanding and enlightenment that could change the course of human history forever.

Shadows of Ancient Prophecies

As they stood on the brink of a discovery that could shake the very foundations of the world, the group sensed the shadows of ancient prophecies and forgotten warnings. The prophecies foretold a time of darkness, forgotten traditions, and lost wisdom.

They realized these prophecies were not just mere predictions or foretelling, but a powerful testament to the enduring power of fate itself. They knew that if they could heed these warnings and embrace the wisdom of the past, they would hold the key to unlocking a new era of hope and renewal that could change the course of human destiny forever.

Unraveling the Threads of Mythology

As they stood amidst the ancient ruins, the group realized that the threads of mythology and legend they had uncovered were not just mere stories or tales, but a powerful testament to the enduring power of the human spirit. They knew that if they could unravel these threads and weave them into a new tapestry of understanding, they would hold the key to unlocking a new era of wisdom and enlightenment.

They discovered that the mythology they had uncovered was not just a mere collection of stories or legends, but a living testament to the enduring power of the imagination itself. They knew that if they could embrace this power and share it with the world, they would hold the key to unlocking a new era of creativity and wonder that could change the course of human history forever.

The Legacy of Myth in Modern Society

As they emerged from the timeless realm, the group realized that the legacy of myth and legend they had uncovered was not just a mere relic of the past, but a powerful force that continued to shape and influence the modern world. They saw echoes of the ancient stories in the books they read, the movies they watched, and the games they played, and they knew that the power of myth was still very much alive and well.

They realized this legacy was not just a mere curiosity or oddity, but a powerful testament to the enduring power of the human imagination. They knew that if they could embrace this legacy and share it with the world, they would hold the key to unlocking a new era of creativity and wonder that could change the course of human history forever.

The Mythic Quest for Truth

As they reflected on their journey, the group realized that their quest for truth and understanding was not just a mere academic pursuit, but a powerful testament to the enduring power of the human spirit. They knew that if they could continue to seek the mysteries of the past and the secrets of the universe, they would hold the key to unlocking a new era of wisdom and enlightenment.

They discovered that the quest for truth was not just a mere journey or adventure, but a living testament to the enduring power of the soul itself. They knew that if they could embrace this quest and share it with the world, they would hold the key to unlocking a new era of peace and harmony that could change the course of human destiny forever.

Reflections on the Eternal Power of the Past

As they stood on the brink of a new era, the group realized that the power of the past was not just a mere memory or echo, but a living force that continued to shape and influence the world around them. Understanding and appreciating the wisdom of the ages would be possible if they could honor and respect this power, as they knew.

They discovered the past was not just a mere collection of stories or legends, but a powerful testament to the enduring power of the human spirit. By embracing this power and sharing it with the world, they knew they would hold the key to unlocking a new era of hope and renewal that could change the course of human history forever.

Part IV: Conclusion and Reflections

The Haunting Echoes of Ancient Whispers

As they looked back on their journey, the group realized that the haunting echoes of ancient whispers they had encountered were not just mere figments of their imagination, but a powerful testament to the enduring power of the past. They knew that if they could continue to listen to these whispers and unravel their secrets, they would hold the key to unlocking a new era of understanding and enlightenment.

They discovered that the whispers of the past were not just mere sounds or noises, but a living testament to the enduring power of the human spirit. They knew that if they could embrace these whispers and share them with the world, they would hold the key to unlocking a new era of wisdom and understanding that could change the course of human history forever.

Shadows of the Past: A Reflection on Timeless Truths

As they reflected on the shadows of the past they had encountered, the group realized these shadows were not just mere absences of light, but a powerful testament to the enduring power of truth itself. They knew that if they could continue to seek these shadows and illuminate their secrets, they would hold the key to unlocking a new era of understanding and enlightenment.

They discovered that the shadows of the past were not just mere mysteries or enigmas, but a living testament to the enduring power of the human spirit. They knew that if they could embrace these shadows and share them with the world, they would hold the key to unlocking a new era of wisdom and understanding that could change the course of human history forever.

Unearthing the Lost Wisdom of Forgotten Civilizations

As they looked back on the lost wisdom of forgotten civilizations they had unearthed, the group realized that this wisdom was not just a mere relic of the past, but a powerful testament to the enduring power of knowledge itself. They knew that if they could continue to seek this wisdom and share it with the world, they would hold the key to unlocking a new era of understanding and enlightenment.

They discovered that the lost wisdom of forgotten civilizations was not just a mere collection of facts or figures, but a living testament to the enduring power of the human spirit. They knew that if they could embrace this wisdom and share it with the world, they would hold the key to unlocking a new era of hope and renewal that could change the course of human history forever.

The Enigmatic Threads That Bind History Together

As they reflected on the enigmatic threads that bound history together, the group realized these threads were not just mere coincidences or happenstances, but a powerful testament to the enduring power of fate itself. They knew that if they could continue to unravel these threads and follow their path, they would hold the key to unlocking a new era of understanding and enlightenment.

They discovered that the threads of history were not just mere connections or links, but a living testament to the enduring power of the human spirit. They knew that if they could embrace these threads and share them with the world, they would hold the key to unlocking a new era of wisdom and understanding that could change the course of human destiny forever.

Delving into the Depths of Historical Mysteries

As they looked back on the depths of historical mysteries they had delved into, the group realized these mysteries were not just mere puzzles or riddles, but a powerful testament to the enduring power of curiosity itself. They knew that if they could continue to explore these mysteries and unravel their secrets, they would hold the key to unlocking a new era of discovery and wonder.

They discovered that the depths of historical mysteries were not just mere unknowns or uncertainties, but a living testament to the enduring power of the human spirit. They knew that if they could embrace these mysteries and share them with the world, they would hold the key to unlocking a new era of exploration and adventure that could change the course of human history forever.

Lessons Learned Through the Veil of Secrecy

As they reflected on the lessons they had learned through the veil of secrecy, the group realized these lessons were not just mere insights or revelations, but a powerful testament to the enduring power of truth itself. Knowing that seeking the truth and sharing it with the world held the key to a new era of understanding and enlightenment, they were determined to continue.

They discovered the lessons learned through the veil of secrecy were not just mere knowledge or information, but a living testament to the enduring power of the human spirit. They knew that if they could embrace these lessons and share them with the world, they would hold the key to unlocking a new era of wisdom and understanding that could change the course of human destiny forever.

Illuminating the Path Forward with Ancient Knowledge

As they looked to the future, the group realized that the ancient knowledge they had uncovered was not just a mere relic of the past, but a powerful tool for illuminating the path forward. Recognizing that by persistently pursuing this knowledge and implementing it in present-day challenges, they understood they possessed the means to unlock a fresh era of progress and enlightenment.

Upon their discovery of ancient knowledge, they realized it was not just a mere collection of facts or figures, but a living testament to the enduring power of the human spirit. They knew that if they could embrace this knowledge and share it with the world, they would hold the key to unlocking a new era of hope and renewal that could change the course of human history forever.

Echoes of the Past: A Call to Uncover Hidden Truths

As they stood on the brink of a new era, the group realized that the echoes of the past they had encountered were not just mere whispers or murmurs, but a powerful call to action. They knew that if they could continue to listen to these echoes and follow their lead, they would hold the key to uncovering the hidden truths that could change the world.

They discovered that the echoes of the past were not just mere sounds or noises, but a living testament to the enduring power of the human spirit. They knew that if they could embrace these echoes and share them with the world, they would hold the key to unlocking a new era of discovery and wonder that could change the course of human destiny forever.

The Mysterious Legacy of the Kincaid Conspiracy

As they reflected on the mysterious legacy of the Kincaid Conspiracy, the group realized this legacy was not just a mere footnote in history, but a powerful testament to the enduring power of mystery itself. They knew that if they could continue to explore this legacy and unravel its secrets, they would hold the key to unlocking a new era of understanding and enlightenment.

They discovered that the legacy of the Kincaid Conspiracy was not just a mere story or tale, but a living testament to the enduring power of the human spirit. They knew that if they could embrace this legacy and share it with the world, they would hold the key to unlocking a new era of wonder and imagination that could change the course of human history forever.

Reflections on the Enigmatic Journey Through History

As they looked back on their enigmatic journey through history, the group realized this journey was not just a mere adventure or quest, but a powerful testament to the enduring power of the human spirit. Holding the key to unlocking a new era of discovery and wonder, they knew they could continue to embark on such journeys and explore the mysteries of the past.

They discovered that the enigmatic journey through history was not just a mere trip or voyage, but a living testament to the enduring power of curiosity itself. Understanding that embracing this journey and sharing it with the world would give them the key to unlock a new era of exploration and adventure, which had the potential to shape the course of human destiny forever.

Lessons Learned in the Depths of History

The Whispers of the Past: Unearthing Hidden Truths

As they reflected on the whispers of the past they had encountered, the group realized these whispers were not just mere echoes or reverberations, but a powerful testament to the enduring power of truth itself. They knew that if they could continue to listen to these whispers and unearth their hidden truths, they would hold the key to unlocking a new era of understanding and enlightenment.

They discovered that the whispers of the past were not just mere sounds or noises, but a living testament to the enduring power of the human spirit. They knew that if they could embrace these whispers and share them with the world, they would hold the key to unlocking a new era of wisdom and understanding that could change the course of human history forever.

Echoes of Ancient Civilizations: Decoding Lost Knowledge

As they looked back on the echoes of ancient civilizations they had encountered, the group realized these were not just mere remnants or relics, but a powerful testament to the enduring power of knowledge itself. Unlocking a new era of discovery and fascination was within their grasp if they could persevere in deciphering these echoes and revealing their hidden knowledge.

Researchers found that the echoes of ancient civilizations were not mere artifacts or ruins. They knew that if they could embrace these echoes and share them with the world, they would hold the key to unlocking a new era of wisdom and understanding that could change the course of human destiny forever.

The Footsteps of Giants: Tracing the Legacy of Kincaid's Discovery

As they reflected on the giants' footsteps they had traced, the group realized these footsteps were not mere tracks or trails, but a powerful testament to the enduring power of discovery itself. They believed that by following in Kincaid's footsteps and continuing his legacy, they would unlock a new era of exploration and adventure.

The discovery revealed that the footsteps of giants were more than just imprints or impressions; they were a living testament to the enduring power of the human spirit. They knew that if they could embrace these footsteps and share them with the world, they would hold the key to unlocking a new era of wonder and imagination that could change the course of human history forever.

Shadows of Betrayal: Uncovering the Price of Secrets

As they looked back on the shadows of betrayal they had encountered, the group realized these shadows were not just mere deceptions or lies, but a powerful testament to the enduring power of secrets themselves. They knew that if they could continue to uncover these shadows and reveal their hidden costs, they would hold the key to unlocking a new era of transparency and accountability.

The Veil of Deception: Lessons in Truth and Illusion

As the ancient whispers of betrayal echo through the corridors of time, a veil of deception shrouds the truths hidden beneath the surface. Illusions dance on the edges of reality, tempting seekers with tantalizing half-truths and veiled lies. The price of secrets is steep, paid in the currency of trust and betrayal, leaving scars on the fabric of history that may never fully heal.

Deception reveals hidden truths and messes with reality. By presenting alternative perspectives, it challenges our perception of truth and forces us to reevaluate our beliefs. We must carefully navigate through the web of lies and always question what meets the eye, for hidden truths and unresolved enigmas lie beneath the surface.

Amidst the darkness, a faint flicker of light emerges, illuminating our path through the treacherous waters of deception. The illusions that once clouded our vision dissolve, revealing glimpses of the hidden truths that lie beyond. In this dance of shadows and light, we learn to see through the veils of deception, embracing the mysteries that bind us to the echoes of the past.

Throughout history, truth and illusion have intertwined, creating a complex tapestry of understanding. Peeling back the layer of deception reveals hidden lessons and deepens our understanding of the interplay between reality and illusion. When on the verge of discovery, deception can only temporarily mask the truth until knowledge uncovers everything.

Echoes Across Time: Reflections on Historical Resonance

Whispers carried by the winds of time drift through the corridors of history, echoing the secrets of the past. In the shadows of forgotten tombs and crumbling ruins, the voices of ancient civilizations beckon us to listen, to unravel the tapestry of time that binds us to them. As we stand on the precipice of a world long gone, we feel the weight of ages pressing down upon us, a reminder of the fleeting nature of human existence.

The ruins we explore and the artifacts we unearth are not mere remnants of a bygone era; they are living echoes of a time long past, resonating with the dreams and aspirations of those who came before us. Each discovery carries with it a sense of mystery and wonder, a tantalizing glimpse into a world shrouded in myth and legend.

In the dance of shadows and light, we see glimpses of a reality that transcends the boundaries of time and space. The stone figures and intricate carvings speak to us in a language older than words, a language that stirs something deep within our souls. As we trace the outlines of ancient civilizations, we find ourselves drawn into a web of connections that span the breadth of human history.

Through the lens of archaeology, we come to understand the profound impact that these discoveries have on our understanding of the past. They force us to question our assumptions and challenge our beliefs, inviting us to reexamine the narratives that shape our collective identity. The weight of history bears down upon us, urging us to confront the mysteries that lie buried beneath the layers of time.

As we trace the footsteps of our ancestors, we encounter the delicate nature of human pursuits and the everlasting influence of human determination. The echoes of the past reverberate through the corridors of our minds, reminding us of the eternal quest for knowledge and understanding that binds us together across the ages.

The Weight of History: Understanding the Impact of Archaeological Discoveries

Every artefact excavated from the depths of history carries with it a weight far greater than its physical mass. It holds within its ancient confines the stories of those long gone, whispering secrets of a bygone era. The impact of these archaeological discoveries reverberates through time, connecting us to our ancestors in ways we could never have imagined.

While excavating these remnants of bygone eras, we realize that our journey through time is not solitary. Each fragment represents a part of humanity's collective memory, a fragment of our shared history awaiting assembly. The weight of history bears down upon us, reminding us of the importance of preservation and understanding.

These findings reveal past civilizations and teach us timeless lessons. They serve as a bridge between the past and the present, allowing us to glimpse into the mysteries of ancient cultures and societies. These archaeological treasures give us a deeper understanding of our place in the grand tapestry of human history.

Archaeological discoveries have a profound impact on us, shaping our perspectives and reshaping our narratives. They challenge us to question our assumptions and biases, forcing us to confront the complexities of our shared past. We carry history with reverence, knowing that it holds the key to unlocking the mysteries of our origins and shaping our future.

Illuminating the Unknown: Lessons from Shadows and Light

Shadows dance across the walls of time, casting their enigmatic glow on the depths of history. In the flickering light, secrets long buried stir, whispering tales of forgotten civilizations and ancient wisdom. Here, in the play of shadows and light, we find the hidden lessons of the unknown.

As we explore the enigmas of history further, we face the dichotomy of darkness and illumination. The shadows represent the invisible, the enigmatic verities that escape our understanding. Contained within them are the repercussions of age-old wisdom, awaiting illumination through comprehension.

The flickering light reveals the truth, exposing history and untold stories. We must be careful, though, because finding the right balance between showing and hiding is tricky.

As we unravel the mysteries of the unknown, we must embrace both the shadows and the light, for they are inseparable companions on the journey through time. In their interplay, we find the lessons that guide us toward a deeper understanding of the past and illuminate the path toward a future shaped by the echoes of history.

The Tapestry of Time: Weaving Together Threads of the Past

Within the labyrinth of time's embrace, the threads of history intertwine, forming a tapestry of secrets shrouded in mystery and intrigue. Each thread tells a tale of civilizations lost to the annals of time, whispers of ancient wisdom echoing through the sands of forgotten eras. As we unravel the tapestry of time, we glimpse the enigmatic forces that have shaped our world, hidden from the eyes of the modern age.

Through the lens of the past, we witness a convergence of cultures, a mosaic of beliefs and traditions that have stood the test of time. The intricate patterns woven by our ancestors speak of a deeper connection, a shared heritage that defies the limitations of language and geography. In the shadows of forgotten empires, we find echoes of our existence, reminding us of the fragility of human endeavor in the face of inevitable change.

As we follow the threads of history, we navigate a landscape of intersecting narratives, where myth and reality blur into a tapestry of wondrous and mysterious tales. The ancient empires rose and fell, leaving a legacy of triumphs and tragedies etched into the fabric of time. Through the tapestry of time, we witness the resilience of the human spirit and the enduring quest for knowledge and understanding that transcends the boundaries of ages.

In the weaving together of threads long frayed by the ravages of time, we discover a profound truth: that the tapestry of history is a living entity, ever developing and expanding with each new revelation. As we unravel its intricate patterns and hidden motifs, we understand the interconnectedness of all things, the pulse of life that beats beneath the surface of our collective memory.

The interwoven fabric of time serves as a constant reminder of our responsibility to pay homage to the wisdom imparted by our predecessors, safeguarding their narratives to ensure the unbroken cycle of discovery and remembrance for future generations. In the timeless fabric of history, we find solace and inspiration, a guiding light that leads us through the shadows of uncertainty towards a brighter tomorrow.

The Power of Remembrance: Honoring the Lessons Hidden in History

As the shadows of time dance across the ancient ruins, a whisper of mystery lingers in the air. The stones hold secrets untold, stories of civilizations long forgotten. The power of remembrance echoes through the corridors of history, urging us to listen, to learn, to honor the lessons hidden in the depths of the past.

In the flickering torchlight, the walls come alive with images of a bygone era. Figures in strange attire, symbols of unknown meaning, a language lost to the ages. Every carving holds significance as a puzzle fragment, offering a glimpse into an untold truth. As we trace our fingers along the grooves, we feel the weight of history pressing down upon us, urging us to remember.

The artifacts we unearth are not mere trinkets of the past; they are keys to unlocking the mysteries that lie buried beneath the sands of time. Each pottery shard, each engraved tablet, each piece of ancient jewelry tells a tale of a person long gone, a civilization erased by the march of time. We hold these objects in our hands with a reverence born of understanding, knowing that they are more than just relics - they are windows into the world that once was.

But remembrance is not just about preserving the past; it is about learning from it. The mistakes of those who came before can serve as cautionary tales for our own time. The hubris of empires, the folly of wars, the subjugation of peoples - these are the lessons that history teaches us if only we will listen. As we stand on the precipice of the unknown, we must look back at the footprints left by those who walked before us and heed their warnings.

In the quiet moments of reflection, we understand the power of remembrance. It is not just a duty we owe to the dead; it is a gift we give to ourselves. By honoring the lessons hidden in history, we can shape a better future for generations yet to come. Thus, we are at the edge of time, our gaze fixed on the past, our hearts receptive to the insight that remains.

Legacy of the Kincaid Conspiracy

The Echoes of the Past: Uncovering the Truth

As they delved deeper into the legacy of the Kincaid Conspiracy, the group realized that the echoes of the past they had encountered were not just mere whispers or murmurs, but a powerful testament to the enduring power of truth itself. The key to unlocking a new era of historical understanding and enlightenment lay in their ability to continue uncovering these echoes and bringing their truths to light.

The echoes of the past were a testament to our enduring spirit. They knew that if they could embrace these echoes and share their truths with the world, they would hold the key to unlocking a new era of historical honesty and integrity that could change the course of human destiny forever.

Whispers in the Wind: Rumors and Speculations

As they reflected on the whispers in the wind they had encountered, the group realized these whispers were not just mere rumors or speculations, but a powerful testament to the enduring power of curiosity itself. They knew that if they could continue to follow these whispers and unravel their mysteries, they would hold the key to unlocking a new era of historical discovery and wonder.

Those whispers in the wind? They were a testament to our unbreakable spirit. Embracing these whispers and sharing their mysteries with the world, they knew they would hold the key to unlocking a new era of historical exploration and adventure that could change the course of human destiny forever.

Shadows of Doubt: Questioning Official Narratives

As they looked back on the shadows of doubt they had encountered, the group realized these shadows were not just mere uncertainties or misgivings, but a powerful testament to the enduring power of questioning itself. In knowing that by maintaining the ability to cast these shadows and question official narratives, they held the key to unlocking a new era of historical truth and accountability.

They discovered that the shadows of doubt were not just mere shades or hues, but a living testament to the enduring power of the human spirit. Embracing these shadows and sharing their questions with the world, they knew they could hold the key to unlocking a new era of historical honesty and transparency that could change the course of human destiny forever.

Silent Witnesses: Untold Tales and Unseen Artifacts

As they reflected on the silent witnesses they had encountered, the group realized these witnesses were not just mere observers or spectators, but a powerful testament to the enduring power of untold tales and unseen artifacts themselves. The key to unlocking a new era of historical richness and diversity lay in their ability to continue uncovering these witnesses and bringing their stories to light.

The silent witnesses, as discovered by them, were not just mere presences or absences, but a living testament to the enduring power of the human spirit. They knew that if they could embrace these witnesses and share their tales with the world, they would hold the key to unlocking a new era of historical inclusivity and representation that could change the course of human destiny forever.

The Veil of Secrecy: Unraveling Hidden Agendas

As they delved deeper into the veil of secrecy that surrounded the Kincaid Conspiracy, the group realized this veil was not just a mere curtain or shroud, but a powerful testament to the enduring power of hidden agendas themselves. They knew that if they could continue to unravel this veil and expose the agendas behind it, they would hold the key to unlocking a new era of historical transparency and accountability.

They discovered that the veil of secrecy was not just a mere cover or concealment, but a living testament to the enduring power of the human spirit. They knew that if they could embrace this veil and share its secrets with the world, they would hold the key to unlocking a new era of historical honesty and openness that could change the course of human destiny forever.

A Trail of Clues: Following the Footsteps of Kincaid

As they reflected on the trail of clues they had followed, the group realized this trail was not just a mere path or route, but a powerful testament to the enduring power of Kincaid's legacy itself. They knew that if they could continue to follow this trail and uncover its secrets, they would hold the key to unlocking a new era of historical discovery and exploration.

They discovered that the trail of clues was not just a mere series of signs or markers, but a living testament to the enduring power of the human spirit. They knew that if they could embrace this trail and share its wonders with the world, they would hold the key to unlocking a new era of historical adventure and excitement that could change the course of human destiny forever.

Lost in Time: The Enigma of Ancient Civilizations

As they looked back on the ancient civilizations they had encountered, the group realized these civilizations were not just mere societies or cultures, but a powerful testament to the enduring power of human ingenuity and creativity itself. They knew that if they could continue to study these civilizations and unravel their mysteries, they would hold the key to unlocking a new era of historical understanding and appreciation.

They found out that the ancient civilizations were not just leftovers, but proof that the human spirit was unstoppable. Embracing these civilizations and sharing their wonders with the world, they knew they held the key to unlocking a new era of historical awe and inspiration that could change the course of human destiny forever.

Uncovering the Forbidden: Forbidden Knowledge and Hidden Truths

As they reflected on the forbidden knowledge and hidden truths they had uncovered, the group realized these secrets were not just mere facts or information, but a powerful testament to the enduring power of human curiosity and the quest for truth itself. They knew that if they could continue to uncover these secrets and bring their truths to light, they would hold the key to unlocking a new era of historical enlightenment and liberation.

The forbidden knowledge and hidden truths were alive, showing the incredible power of the human spirit. They knew that if they could embrace these secrets and share their truths with the world, they would hold the key to unlocking a new era of historical freedom and empowerment that could change the course of human destiny forever.

The Legacy Lives On: Impact on Modern Beliefs and Understanding

As they stood on the brink of a new era of historical understanding, the group realized that the legacy of the Kincaid Conspiracy was not just a mere memory or record, but a powerful testament to the enduring power of historical impact itself. Recognizing that preserving this heritage and disseminating its teachings would be crucial, they understood they held the key to ushering in a new era of historical wisdom and enlightenment that could forever alter contemporary beliefs and comprehension.

The discovery revealed that the legacy of the Kincaid Conspiracy went beyond being a simple story or tale—it was a living testament to the unwavering strength of the human spirit. They knew that if they could embrace this legacy and share its impact with the world, they would hold the key to unlocking a new era of historical appreciation and gratitude that could shape the beliefs and understanding of generations to come.

The Final Revelation: Challenging Perspectives and Embracing Discovery

As they stood on the precipice of a new era of historical discovery, the group realized that the last revelation of the Kincaid Conspiracy was not just a mere conclusion or ending, but a powerful testament to the enduring power of challenging perspectives and embracing discovery itself. They knew that if they could continue to challenge their own perspectives and embrace new discoveries, they would hold the key to unlocking a new era of historical enlightenment and transformation.

The last revelation, they found, was more than a mere outcome or result—it was a living testament to the enduring power of the human spirit. They knew that if they could embrace this revelation and share its challenges and discoveries with the world, they would hold the key to unlocking a new era of historical wonder and excitement that could transform the way we see the world and our place in it forever.

Appendices and Resources

Cryptic Testimonies and Hidden Clues

As they delved deeper into the appendices and resources related to the Kincaid Conspiracy, the group realized that the cryptic testimonies and hidden clues they had uncovered were not just mere statements or hints, but a powerful testament to the enduring power of historical evidence. With their ability to uncover these testimonies and clues and connect their meanings, they knew they held the key to unlocking a new era of historical understanding and insight.

The cryptic testimonies and hidden clues they found were more than just mere words or phrases; they were a living testament to the enduring power of the human spirit. They knew that if they could embrace these testimonies and clues and share their meanings with the world, they would hold the key to unlocking a new era of historical discovery and exploration that could change the way we see the past and our connection to it forever.

The Enigmatic Language of Ancient Documents

As they reflected on the enigmatic language of the ancient documents they had encountered, the group realized that this language was not just a mere code or cipher, but a powerful testament to the enduring power of historical communication itself. Holding the key to unlocking a new era of historical understanding and appreciation, they knew that if they could continue to decipher this language and unravel its meanings.

The discovery revealed that the enigmatic language of ancient documents was not simply a mere system or structure, but a living testament to the enduring power of the human spirit. Recognizing that by embracing this language and sharing its meanings with the world, they could unlock a new era of historical connection and empathy, forever altering our relationships with the past and each other.

Uncovering Secrets in Forgotten Manuscripts

As they looked back on the secrets they had uncovered in forgotten manuscripts, the group realized these secrets were not just mere facts or information, but a powerful testament to the enduring power of historical preservation itself. Knowing that by persistently uncovering these secrets and revealing their truths, they held the key to ushering in a new era of historical recovery and restoration.

Uncovering the secrets within forgotten manuscripts revealed more than just mere data or evidence, but a living testament to the enduring power of the human spirit. They knew that if they could embrace these secrets and share their truths with the world, they would hold the key to unlocking a new era of historical reverence and respect that could change the way we value and protect the past forever.

Illustrated Mysteries: Symbols and Significance

As they reflected on the illustrated mysteries and symbols they had encountered, the group realized that these mysteries and symbols were not just mere pictures or designs, but a powerful testament to the enduring power of historical art and expression itself. They knew that if they could continue to study these mysteries and symbols and unravel their meanings, they would hold the key to unlocking a new era of historical creativity and inspiration.

They discovered that the illustrated mysteries and symbols were not mere images or graphics, but a living testament to the enduring power of the human spirit. They knew that if they could embrace these mysteries and symbols and share their meanings with the world, they would be the key to unlocking a new era of historical artistry and innovation that could forever change how we express and communicate with the past.

Beyond the Surface: Deeper Meanings Revealed

As the group delved deeper into the meanings uncovered by the Kincaid Conspiracy, they realized that these were not just interpretations or explanations, but a powerful testament to the enduring power of historical insight and revelation. They understood that by consistently revealing these meanings and sharing their truths, they would hold the key to unlocking a new era of historical knowledge and enlightenment. They discovered that there were deeper meanings beyond mere conclusions or summaries.

Lost Knowledge: Scrolls and Scrolls of Ages Past

As they reflected on the lost knowledge and ancient scrolls they had uncovered, the group realized that this knowledge and these scrolls were not just mere information or documents, but a powerful testament to the enduring power of historical wisdom and learning itself. Knowing that by continuing to uncover this knowledge and these scrolls and sharing their truths with the world, they would have the power to unlock a new era of historical education and enlightenment.

Those mundane facts about lost knowledge and ancient scrolls turned out to be really fascinating. They knew that if they could embrace this knowledge and these scrolls and share their truths with the world, they would be the key to unlocking a new era of historical curiosity and discovery that could forever change how we learn and grow from the past.

The Veil of Secrecy Lifted: Revelations in Textual Analysis

As they delved deeper into the veil of secrecy lifted by their textual analysis, the group realized these revelations were not just mere findings or conclusions, but a powerful testament to the enduring power of historical research and investigation itself. They knew that if they could continue to lift this veil and uncover these revelations, they would hold the key to unlocking a new era of historical truth and transparency.

The findings in textual analysis were more than plain results. They knew that if they could embrace these revelations and share their truths with the world, they would hold the key to unlocking a new era of historical honesty and integrity that could forever change how we seek and share the truth.

Anomalies in the Archives: Unexplained Phenomena

As they reflected on the anomalies and unexplained phenomena they had encountered in the archives, the group realized that these anomalies and phenomena were not just mere oddities or curiosities, but a powerful testament to the enduring power of historical mystery and wonder itself. Understanding that by persisting in studying these anomalies and phenomena and unraveling their secrets, they could unlock a new era of historical awe and inspiration.

What they found in the archives went beyond mere irregularities or deviations; it was a living testament to the enduring power of the human spirit. They knew that if they could embrace these anomalies and share their secrets with the world, they would be the key to unlocking a new era of historical curiosity and exploration that could forever change how we marvel at and appreciate the past.

Shadows of Truth: Uncovering the Hidden Narratives

As they delved deeper into the shadows of truth and the hidden narratives they had uncovered, the group realized that these shadows and narratives were not just mere secrets or stories, but a powerful testament to the enduring power of historical perspective and understanding itself. Knowing that by continuing to uncover these shadows and narratives and sharing their truths with the world, they would hold the key to unlocking a new era of historical empathy and compassion.

We realized that the shadows of truth and hidden narratives are living proof of the incredible strength of the human spirit. They knew that if they could embrace these shadows and narratives and share their truths with the world, they would be the key to unlocking a new era of historical connection and healing that could change how we relate to and learn from the past forever.

Paths to Enlightenment: Further Reading and Exploration

As they stood on the brink of a new era of historical understanding and appreciation, the group realized that the paths to enlightenment and further reading and exploration that lay before them were not just mere options or choices, but a powerful testament to the enduring power of historical curiosity and discovery itself. Recognizing that if they persisted in following these paths and seizing these opportunities for further learning and growth, they might forever alter the trajectory of human knowledge and understanding, unlocking a new era of historical wisdom and insight.

In their discovery, the paths to enlightenment and further reading and exploration were more than mere routes or directions; they were a vibrant, living testament to the everlasting strength of the human spirit. They knew that if they could embrace these paths and share their discoveries with the world, they would hold the key to unlocking a new era of historical wonder and excitement that could inspire and transform future generations.

Appendix A: Deciphering Documents and Testimonies

The Cryptic Scrolls: Unraveling Ancient Texts

As they delved deeper into the appendix on deciphering documents and testimonies, the group realized that the cryptic scrolls and ancient texts they had uncovered were not just mere writings or inscriptions, but a powerful testament to the enduring power of historical language and communication. They knew that if they could continue to unravel these scrolls and texts and decipher their meanings, they would hold the key to unlocking a new era of historical understanding and appreciation.

They discovered that the cryptic scrolls and ancient texts were not just mere documents or records, but a living testament to the enduring power of the human spirit. They knew that if they could embrace these scrolls and texts and share their meanings with the world, they would hold the key to unlocking a new era of historical connection and empathy that could change the way we relate to and learn from the past forever.

The Testaments of Time: Historical Accounts and Enigmatic Testimonies

As they reflected on the testaments of time and the historical accounts and enigmatic testimonies they had uncovered, the group realized that these testaments and testimonies were not mere stories or narratives, but powerful testaments to the enduring power of historical perspective and understanding itself. They knew that if they could continue studying these testaments and testimonies and unraveling their secrets, they would be the key to unlocking a new era of historical empathy and compassion.

The testaments of time, historical accounts, and enigmatic testimonies were more than just mere facts or fictions; they were a living testament to the enduring power of the human spirit. They knew that if they could embrace these testaments and testimonies and share their secrets with the world, they would hold the key to unlocking a new era of historical connection and healing that could change the way we relate to and learn from the past forever.

The Puzzle Pieces: Connecting Clues and Contradictions

As they delved deeper into the puzzle pieces and the clues and contradictions they had uncovered, the group realized these puzzle pieces and clues and contradictions were not just mere facts or fictions, but a powerful testament to the enduring power of historical research and investigation itself. They knew that if they could continue to connect these puzzle pieces and unravel these clues and contradictions, they would hold the key to unlocking a new era of historical truth and transparency.

They discovered the puzzle pieces and clues and contradictions were not just mere results or outcomes, but a living testament to the enduring power of the human spirit. They knew that if they could embrace these puzzle pieces, clues, and contradictions and share their truths with the world, they would hold the key to unlocking a new era of historical honesty and integrity that could change the way we seek and share the truth forever.

Voices from the Past: Echoes of Mystery in Old Documents

As they reflected on the voices from the past and the echoes of mystery they had encountered in old documents, the group realized that these voices and echoes were not just mere sounds or vibrations, but a powerful testament to the enduring power of historical communication and expression itself. Unraveling the meanings of these voices and echoes would allow them to hold the key to a new era of historical understanding and appreciation they knew.

The discovery revealed that the voices of the past and the mysteries hidden in old documents were more than just sounds or echoes; they were a testament to the everlasting strength of the human spirit. Embracing these voices and echoes, they knew that sharing their meanings with the world held the key to unlocking a new era of historical connection and empathy, forever changing the way we relate to and learn from the past.

The Hidden Codes: Cracking the Secrets of Symbolism

As they delved deeper into the hidden codes and the secrets of symbolism they had uncovered, the group realized that these codes and secrets were not just mere ciphers or puzzles, but a powerful testament to the enduring power of historical meaning and significance itself. They knew that if they could continue to crack these codes and unravel these secrets, they would hold the key to unlocking a new era of historical understanding and appreciation.

They discovered that the hidden codes and secrets of symbolism were not just mere signs or symbols, but a living testament to the enduring power of the human spirit. They knew that if they could embrace these codes and secrets and share their meanings with the world, they would be the key to unlocking a new era of historical connection and empathy that could change how we relate to and learn from the past forever.

Witnesses to History: Accounts of Eyewitnesses and Participants

As they reflected on the witnesses to history and the accounts of eyewitnesses and participants they had uncovered, the group realized that these witnesses and accounts were not just mere observations or descriptions but a powerful testament to the enduring power of historical experience and perspective itself. By continuing to study these witnesses and accounts and unraveling their secrets, they knew they held the key to unlocking a new era of historical empathy and compassion.

The discovery revealed that the witnesses to history and their stories were powerful demonstrations of the resilience of the human spirit. They knew that if they could embrace these witnesses and accounts and share their secrets with the world, they would be the key to unlocking a new era of historical connection and healing that could change how we relate to and learn from the past forever.

The Missing Pages: Uncovering Lost Texts and Forgotten Accounts

As they delved deeper into the missing pages and the lost texts and forgotten accounts they had uncovered, the group realized that these pages and texts and accounts were not just mere documents or records, but a powerful testament to the enduring power of historical preservation and recovery itself. Understanding that by persistently uncovering these pages, texts, and accounts and bringing their truths to light, they could unlock a new era of historical understanding and appreciation.

Upon their discovery, the missing pages, lost texts, and forgotten accounts were more than mere facts or figures; they represented a living testament to the enduring power of the human spirit. They knew that if they could embrace these pages, texts, and accounts and share their truths with the world, they would hold the key to unlocking a new era of historical curiosity and discovery that could change the way we learn and grow from the past forever.

The Language of Mystery: Decoding Untranslatable Scripts

As they reflected on the language of mystery and the untranslatable scripts they had encountered, the group realized that this language and these scripts were not just mere codes or ciphers, but a powerful testament to the enduring power of historical communication and expression itself. The key to unlocking a new era of historical understanding and appreciation lies in their ability to continue decoding this language and these scripts and unraveling their meanings.

The language of mystery and untranslatable scripts, they found, went beyond mere signs or symbols, and embodied the unwavering resilience of the human spirit. They knew that if they could embrace this language and these scripts and share their meanings with the world, they would be the key to unlocking a new era of historical connection and empathy that could change how we relate to and learn from the past forever.

A Tapestry of Truth and Deception: Unveiling Layers of Disinformation

As they delved deeper into the tapestry of truth and deception and the layers of disinformation they had uncovered, the group realized that this tapestry and these layers were not just mere facts or fiction but a powerful testament to the enduring power of historical perspective and understanding itself. They knew that if they could continue to unveil this tapestry and these layers and expose their truths, they would hold the key to unlocking a new era of historical honesty and integrity.

They discovered that the tapestry of truth, deception, and layers of disinformation were not just mere results or outcomes, but a living testament to the enduring power of the human spirit. They knew that if they could embrace this tapestry and these layers and share their truths with the world, they would be the key to unlocking a new era of historical truth and transparency that could change how we seek and share the truth forever.

The Enigma of Interpretation: Seeking Truth Amidst Ambiguity

As they stood on the brink of a new era of historical understanding and appreciation, the group realized that the enigma of interpretation and the search for truth amidst ambiguity that lay before them were not just mere challenges or obstacles, but a powerful testament to the enduring power of historical curiosity and discovery itself. They knew that if they could continue to embrace this enigma and this search and seek the truth in the face of uncertainty and doubt, they would hold the key to unlocking a new era of historical wisdom and insight that could change the course of human knowledge and understanding forever.

They discovered that the enigma of interpretation and the search for truth amidst ambiguity were not just mere difficulties or dilemmas, but a living testament to the enduring power of the human spirit. They knew that if they could embrace this enigma and this search and share their discoveries with the world, they would hold the key to unlocking a new era of historical wonder and excitement that could inspire and transform generations to come.

Appendix B: Illustrations and Insights from the Grand Canyon

Ancient Symbols in Stone

As they delved deeper into the appendix on illustrations and insights from the Grand Canyon, the group realized that the ancient symbols in stone they had uncovered were not just mere carvings or engravings, but a powerful testament to the enduring power of historical art and expression itself. By continuing to study these symbols and unravel their meanings, they knew they would hold the key to unlocking a new era of historical creativity and inspiration.

They discovered that the ancient symbols in stone were not just mere images or graphics but a living testament to the enduring power of the human spirit. They knew that if they could embrace these symbols and share their meanings with the world, they would hold the key to unlocking a new era of historical artistry and innovation that could change the way we express and communicate the past forever.

Whispers of the Past: Petroglyphs and Pictographs

As they reflected on the whispers of the past and the petroglyphs and pictographs they had encountered, the group realized that these whispers and these petroglyphs and pictographs were not just mere sounds or images, but a powerful testament to the enduring power of historical communication and expression itself. They knew that if they could continue to listen to these whispers and study these petroglyphs and pictographs and unravel their meanings, they would hold the key to unlocking a new era of historical understanding and appreciation.

They discovered that the whispers of the past and petroglyphs and pictographs were not just mere noises or pictures, but a living testament to the enduring power of the human spirit. They knew that if they could embrace these whispers and these petroglyphs and pictographs and share their meanings with the world, they would hold the key to unlocking a new era of historical connection and empathy that could change the way we relate to and learn from the past forever.

The Enigmatic Cave Paintings: A Window to Another Time

As they delved deeper into the enigmatic cave paintings and the window to another time they had uncovered, the group realized that these paintings and this window were not just mere art or portals, but a powerful testament to the enduring power of historical perspective and understanding itself. Knowing that if they could persist in studying these paintings and gazing through this window to unravel their secrets, they would possess the key to unlocking a new era of historical empathy and compassion.

The cave paintings and time portal turned out to be more than just fact or fiction. They knew that if they could embrace these paintings and this window and share their secrets with the world, they would hold the key to unlocking a new era of historical connection and healing that could change the way we relate to and learn from the past forever.

Sculptures of Mystery: Uncovering Ancient Artifacts

As they reflected on the sculptures of mystery and the ancient artifacts they had uncovered, the group realized that these sculptures and artifacts were not just mere objects or relics, but a powerful testament to the enduring power of historical preservation and recovery itself. Uncovering these sculptures and artifacts and bringing their stories to light, they knew they would hold the key to unlocking a new era of historical understanding and appreciation.

The discovery revealed that the sculptures of mystery and ancient artifacts were more than just mere items or remnants; they were a living testament to the enduring power of the human spirit. They knew that if they could embrace these sculptures and artifacts and share their stories with the world, they would hold the key to unlocking a new era of historical curiosity and discovery that could change the way we learn and grow from the past forever.

The Cryptic Language of Statues and Carvings

As they delved deeper into the cryptic language of statues and carvings they had encountered, the group realized that this language and these statues and carvings were not just mere codes or objects, but a powerful testament to the enduring power of historical meaning and significance itself. Understanding that if they could persist in deciphering this language and uncovering the secrets of these statues and carvings, they would possess the key to unlocking a new era of historical understanding and appreciation.

Not only were the signs and symbols of statues and carvings discovered to be a cryptic language, but they also represented a living testament to the everlasting resilience of the human spirit. They knew that if they could embrace this language and these statues and carvings and share their meanings with the world, they would hold the key to unlocking a new era of historical connection and empathy that could change the way we relate to and learn from the past forever.

Sacred Sites and Their Secrets

As they reflected on the sacred sites and the secrets they had uncovered, the group realized that these sites and secrets were not just mere places or mysteries, but a powerful testament to the enduring power of historical reverence and respect itself. By continuing to study these sites and unravel their secrets, they knew they would hold the key to unlocking a new era of historical understanding and appreciation.

The revelation came when they realized that the sacred sites and their secrets were not simply physical locations or unsolved riddles, but a dynamic testimony to the unwavering resilience of the human spirit. They knew that if they could embrace these sites and secrets and share their meanings with the world, they would be the key to unlocking a new era of historical reverence and respect that could change how we value and protect the past forever.

The Unexplained Structures: Dwellings of the Ancients

As they delved deeper into the unexplained structures and dwellings of the ancients they had uncovered, the group realized that these structures and dwellings were not just mere buildings or homes, but a powerful testament to the enduring power of historical ingenuity and creativity. They knew that if they could continue studying these structures and dwellings and unraveling their secrets, they would be the key to unlocking a new era of historical understanding and appreciation.

They discovered that the ancients' unexplained structures and dwellings were not mere shelters or habitats but living testaments to the enduring power of the human spirit. They knew that if they could embrace these structures and dwellings and share their secrets with the world, they would be the key to unlocking a new era of historical creativity and innovation that could change how we express and communicate the past forever.

Eerie Echoes of Ancient Rituals: Ceremonial Grounds

As they reflected on the eerie echoes of ancient rituals and the ceremonial grounds they had encountered, the group realized that these echoes and grounds were not just mere sounds or places, but a powerful testament to the enduring power of historical reverence and respect itself. By continuing to listen to these echoes, study these grounds, and unravel their secrets, they knew they would hold the key to unlocking a new era of historical understanding and appreciation.

The eerie echoes of ancient rituals and ceremonial grounds were discovered to be not simply noises or locations, but a living testament to the enduring power of the human spirit. They knew that if they could embrace these echoes and grounds and share their secrets with the world, they would be the key to unlocking a new era of historical reverence and respect that could change how we value and protect the past forever.

Depictions of Gods and Legends

As they delved deeper into the depictions of gods and legends they had uncovered, the group realized these depictions were not just mere art or stories, but a powerful testament to the enduring power of historical meaning and significance itself. They knew that if they could continue to study these depictions and unravel their secrets, they would hold the key to unlocking a new era of historical understanding and appreciation.

The depictions of gods and legends were more than just images or tales; they were a living testament to the enduring power of the human spirit, as discovered by them. They knew that if they could embrace these depictions and share their secrets with the world, they would be the key to unlocking a new era of historical connection and empathy that could change how we relate to and learn from the past forever.

Connecting the Dots: Insights Revealed

Right when the group was about to enter a new stage of comprehending and valuing history, they found that connecting the various parts revealed meaningful insights. These insights were not simple conclusions or summaries, but a powerful testament to the lasting impact of curiosity and discovery in history. They understood that by making connections and discovering new insights, they could gain access to a wealth of historical knowledge and understanding that could have a profound impact on human knowledge.

They discovered that finding connections between different things revealed inspiring insights that showed the enduring resilience of human beings. They knew that if they could embrace these insights and share their discoveries with the world, they would hold the key to unlocking a new era of historical wonder and excitement that could inspire and transform generations to come.

Glossary of Enigmatic Terms

Whispers of the Ancients

As they delved deeper into the glossary of enigmatic terms, the group realized that the ancients' whispers were not mere sounds or echoes, but a powerful testament to the enduring power of historical communication and expression. They knew that if they could continue to listen to these whispers and unravel their meanings, they would hold the key to unlocking a new era of historical understanding and appreciation.

They discovered that the ancients' whispers were not mere noises or reverberations, but a living testament to the enduring power of the human spirit. They knew that if they could embrace these whispers and share their meanings with the world, they would hold the key to unlocking a new era of historical connection and empathy that could change the way we relate to and learn from the past forever.

Cryptic Symbols and Their Meaning

As they reflected on the cryptic symbols and their meanings they had uncovered, the group realized that these symbols and meanings were not just mere signs or definitions, but a powerful testament to the enduring power of historical meaning and significance itself. Understanding that by persisting in studying these symbols and uncovering their meanings, they would gain the key to unlocking a new epoch of historical understanding and appreciation.

They discovered that the cryptic symbols and their meanings were not just mere images or explanations, but a living testament to the enduring power of the human spirit. They knew that if they could embrace these symbols and meanings and share their secrets with the world, they would be the key to unlocking a new era of historical connection and empathy that could change how we relate to and learn from the past forever.

Shadows of the Unknown

As they delved deeper into the shadows of the unknown, the group realized these shadows were not just mere absences or voids, but a powerful testament to the enduring power of historical mystery and wonder itself. The key to unlocking a new era of historical understanding and appreciation lies in their ability to continue exploring these shadows and unraveling their secrets.

The discovery revealed that the shadows of the unknown were more than mere darkness or emptiness; instead, they embodied a living testament to the enduring power of the human spirit. They knew that if they could embrace these shadows and share their secrets with the world, they would hold the key to unlocking a new era of historical curiosity and discovery that could change the way we learn and grow from the past forever.

Secrets of the Mysterious Language

As they reflected on the secrets of the mysterious language they had uncovered, the group realized that these secrets and this language were not just mere codes or ciphers, but a powerful testament to the enduring power of historical communication and expression itself. Recognizing that by continuing to decode these secrets and uncover the meanings of this language, they would gain the ability to unlock a new era of historical understanding and appreciation.

Uncovering the secrets of the mysterious language, they realized it was not merely a collection of puzzles or riddles, but a living testament to the resilience of the human spirit. They knew that if they could embrace these secrets and this language and share their meanings with the world, they would hold the key to unlocking a new era of historical connection and empathy that could change the way we relate to and learn from the past forever.

Unveiling the Mystical Vocabulary

As they delved deeper into the mystical vocabulary they had uncovered, the group realized that this vocabulary was not just mere words or terms, but a powerful testament to the enduring power of historical meaning and significance itself. They knew that if they could continue to unveil this vocabulary and unravel its secrets, they would hold the key to unlocking a new era of historical understanding and appreciation.

They discovered that the mystical vocabulary was not just mere language or jargon, but a living testament to the enduring power of the human spirit. They knew that if they could embrace this vocabulary and share its secrets with the world, they would hold the key to unlocking a new era of historical connection and empathy that could change the way we relate to and learn from the past forever.

Enigmatic Objects and Their Significance

As they reflected on the enigmatic objects and their significance they had uncovered, the group realized that these objects and their significance were not just mere items or meanings, but a powerful testament to the enduring power of historical preservation and recovery itself. They knew that if they could continue to study these objects and unravel their significance, they would hold the key to unlocking a new era of historical understanding and appreciation.

They discovered that the enigmatic objects and their significance were not just mere artifacts or interpretations, but a living testament to the enduring power of the human spirit. They knew that if they could embrace these objects and their significance and share their stories with the world, they would hold the key to unlocking a new era of historical curiosity and discovery that could change the way we learn and grow from the past forever.

The Esoteric Code of the Past

As they delved deeper into the esoteric code of the past, the group realized that this code was not just a mere cipher or puzzle, but a powerful testament to the enduring power of historical meaning and significance itself. They knew that if they could continue to decipher this code and unravel its secrets, they would hold the key to unlocking a new era of historical understanding and appreciation.

They discovered that the esoteric code of the past was not just a mere system or structure, but a living testament to the enduring power of the human spirit. They knew that if they could embrace this code and share its secrets with the world, they would hold the key to unlocking a new era of historical connection and empathy that could change the way we relate to and learn from the past forever.

Lost Words and Forgotten Meanings

As they reflected on the lost words and forgotten meanings they had uncovered, the group realized that these words and meanings were not just mere language or definitions, but a powerful testament to the enduring power of historical communication and expression itself. Holding the key to unlocking a new era of historical understanding and appreciation, they knew that by continuing to rediscover these words and meanings and bringing their truths to light.

They discovered that the lost words and forgotten meanings were not just mere sounds or explanations, but a living testament to the enduring power of the human spirit. They knew that if they could embrace these words and meanings and share their truths with the world, they would hold the key to unlocking a new era of historical curiosity, and discovery could forever change how we learn and grow from the past.

Echoes of a Lost Civilization

As they delved deeper into the echoes of a lost civilization they had encountered, the group realized that these were not just mere sounds or reverberations but a powerful testament to the enduring power of historical preservation and recovery. They knew that if they could continue to listen to these echoes and unravel their secrets, they would hold the key to unlocking a new era of historical understanding and appreciation.

They discovered that the echoes of a lost civilization were not mere noises or vibrations, but a living testament to the enduring power of the human spirit. They knew that if they could embrace these echoes and share their secrets with the world, they would hold the key to unlocking a new era of historical curiosity and discovery that could forever change the way we learn and grow from the past.

The Enigma of Timeless Language

As they stood on the brink of a new era of historical understanding and appreciation, the group realized that the enigma of timeless language that lay before them was not just a mere mystery or puzzle but a powerful testament to the enduring power of historical communication and expression. They knew that if they could continue to explore this enigma and unravel its secrets, they would hold the key to unlocking a new era of historical meaning and significance that could change the course of human understanding and appreciation forever.

They discovered that the timeless language's enigma was not just a mere code or cipher, but a living testament to the enduring power of the human spirit. They knew that if they could embrace this enigma and share its secrets with the world, they would be the key to unlocking a new era of historical connection and empathy that could inspire and transform future generations.

Further Reading for the Curious Seeker

Ancient Texts and Forbidden Knowledge

As they delved deeper into the further reading for the curious seeker, the group realized that the ancient texts and forbidden knowledge they had uncovered were not just mere books or secrets, but a powerful testament to the enduring power of historical wisdom and insight. They knew that if they could continue studying these texts and unraveling their forbidden knowledge, they would be the key to unlocking a new era of historical understanding and appreciation.

They discovered that ancient texts and forbidden knowledge were not mere documents or information, but a living testament to the enduring power of the human spirit. They knew that if they could embrace these texts and knowledge and share their secrets with the world, they would hold the key to unlocking a new era of historical curiosity and discovery that could forever change the way we learn and grow from the past.

Lost Civilizations and Forgotten Realms

As they reflected on the lost civilizations and forgotten realms they had uncovered, the group realized that these civilizations and realms were not mere societies or places but powerful testaments to the enduring power of historical preservation and recovery itself. They knew that by studying these civilizations and realms and uncovering their secrets, they could unlock a new era of historical understanding and appreciation.

The lost civilizations and forgotten realms were more than just cultures or locations; they were living testaments to the enduring power of the human spirit, as discovered by them. They knew that if they could embrace these civilizations and realms and share their secrets with the world, they would hold the key to unlocking a new era of historical curiosity and discovery that could forever change the way we learn and grow from the past.

Cryptic Codes and Unsolved Puzzles

As they delved deeper into the cryptic codes and unsolved puzzles they had encountered, the group realized that these codes and puzzles were not mere ciphers or mysteries, but a powerful testament to the enduring power of historical meaning and significance. They knew that if they could continue deciphering these codes and unravel these puzzles, they would be the key to unlocking a new era of historical understanding and appreciation.

They discovered that the cryptic codes and unsolved puzzles were not just mere systems or structures but a living testament to the enduring power of the human spirit. They knew that if they could embrace these codes and puzzles and share their secrets with the world, they would be the key to unlocking a new era of historical connection and empathy that could change how we relate to and learn from the past forever.

The Occult and Esoteric Wisdom

As they reflected on the occult and esoteric wisdom they had uncovered, the group realized that this wisdom was not just mere knowledge or information, but a powerful testament to the enduring power of historical meaning and significance. They knew that if they could continue studying this wisdom and unraveling its secrets, they would be the key to unlocking a new era of historical understanding and appreciation.

They discovered that occult and esoteric wisdom was not mere beliefs or practices, but a living testament to the enduring power of the human spirit. They knew that if they could embrace this wisdom and share its secrets with the world, they would be the key to unlocking a new era of historical connection and empathy that could forever change how we relate to and learn from the past.

Intriguing Legends and Mythical Lore

As they delved deeper into the intriguing legends and mythical lore they had uncovered, the group realized that these legends and lore were not mere stories or tales, but powerful testaments in the enduring power of historical communication and expression. They knew that if they could continue studying these legends and lore and unraveling their secrets, they would be the key to unlocking a new era of historical understanding and appreciation.

They discovered that the intriguing legends and mythical lore were not mere narratives or folklore, but a living testament to the enduring power of the human spirit. They knew that if they could embrace these legends and lore and share their secrets with the world, they would hold the key to unlocking a new era of historical curiosity and discovery that could forever change the way we learn and grow from the past.

Conspiracy Theories and Hidden Histories

As they reflected on the conspiracy theories and hidden histories they had uncovered, the group realized that these theories and histories were not just mere speculations or secrets but a powerful testament to the enduring power of historical perspective and understanding of itself. They knew that if they could continue exploring these theories and histories and unravel their truths, they would be the key to unlocking a new era of historical honesty and integrity.

They discovered that conspiracy theories and hidden histories were not mere ideas or facts but living testaments to the enduring power of the human spirit. They knew that if they could embrace these theories and histories and share their truths with the world, they would be the key to unlocking a new era of historical fact and transparency that could change how we seek and share the truth forever.

Secret Societies and Clandestine Organizations

As they delved deeper into the secret societies and clandestine organizations they had uncovered, the group realized that these societies and organizations were not mere groups or associations but powerful testaments to the enduring power of historical influence and power itself. They knew that if they could continue studying these societies and organizations and unraveling their secrets, they would be the key to unlocking a new era of historical understanding and appreciation.

They discovered that the secret societies and clandestine organizations were not just mere clubs or fraternities but a living testament to the enduring power of the human spirit. They knew that if they could embrace these societies and organizations and share their secrets with the world, they would be the key to unlocking a new era of historical curiosity and discovery that could change how we learn and grow from the past forever.

Extraterrestrial Encounters and Alien Mysteries

As they reflected on the extraterrestrial encounters and alien mysteries they had uncovered, the group realized that these encounters and mysteries were not mere sightings or phenomena but a powerful testament to the enduring power of historical wonder and imagination. They knew that if they could continue exploring these encounters and mysteries and unravel their secrets, they would be the key to unlocking a new era of historical understanding and appreciation.

They discovered that extraterrestrial encounters and alien mysteries were not mere events or enigmas but living testaments to the enduring power of the human spirit. They knew that if they could embrace these encounters and mysteries and share their secrets with the world, they would hold the key to unlocking a new era of historical curiosity and discovery that could forever change the way we learn and grow from the past.

Occult Practices and Magical Realms

As they delved deeper into the occult practices and magical realms they had uncovered, the group realized that these practices and realms were not mere rituals or places but a powerful testament to the enduring power of historical meaning and significance. They knew that if they could continue studying these practices and realms and unraveling their secrets, they would be the key to unlocking a new era of historical understanding and appreciation.

They discovered that occult practices and magical realms were not mere beliefs or locations but living, breathing testaments to the enduring power of the human spirit. They knew that if they could embrace these practices and realms and share their secrets with the world, they would be the key to unlocking a new era of historical connection and empathy that could forever change how we relate to and learn from the past.

Exploring the Unknown: Journeys of Discovery

As they stood on the brink of a new era of historical understanding and appreciation, the group realized that the journeys of discovery and the exploration of the unknown that lay before them were not just mere adventures or quests but a powerful testament to the enduring power of historical curiosity and wonder itself. They knew that if they could continue to embark on these journeys and embrace the unknown, they would hold the key to unlocking a new era of historical wisdom and insight that could change the course of human knowledge and understanding forever.

They discovered that journeys of discovery and exploration of the unknown were not mere trips or expeditions but living testaments to the enduring power of the human spirit. They knew that if they could embrace these journeys and share their discoveries with the world, they would hold the key to unlocking a new era of historical wonder and excitement that could inspire and transform future generations.

References

Books and Articles

- **Hidden Depths: The Kincaid Conspiracy and The Secrets of The Grand Canyon**
  This book explores the mysteries and conspiracies surrounding the Grand Canyon, including the lost civilizations and enigmatic symbols that have puzzled researchers for generations.

Historical and Archaeological Sources

- **Ancient Symbols and Languages**
  Extensive study has been conducted on the intricate carvings and symbols found within the Grand Canyon. These symbols offer insights into the rituals and beliefs of ancient civilizations that once inhabited the area.
- **The Lost Explorers**
  Accounts of early explorers who ventured into the Grand Canyon, leaving behind cryptic clues and mysterious artifacts that continue to fuel speculation and intrigue.

Research Papers and Journals

- **Journal of Archaeological Mysteries**
  This journal includes various articles on the hidden chambers and ancient relics discovered in the Grand Canyon, discussing their significance and potential connections to other ancient cultures.
- **Historical Enigmas Quarterly**
  A publication dedicated to exploring unresolved historical mysteries, including the theories about G.E. Kincaid's expedition and the hidden

truths it might reveal.

Online Resources and Databases

- **Ancient Civilizations Database**
  An online repository of information on ancient cultures, including detailed analyzes of symbols and artifacts found in the Grand Canyon.
- **Mystery Seekers Forum**
  This is an online community where enthusiasts and researchers discuss the latest findings and theories related to historical mysteries and archaeological discoveries.

Personal Correspondence and Interviews

- **Interview with Dr. Roberts**
  A leading archaeologist who has conducted extensive research on the Grand Canyon's hidden artifacts and symbols, providing expert insights into their potential meanings and implications.

Media and Documentaries

- **Echoes of the Past: The Grand Canyon's Hidden Secrets**
  A documentary that delves into the unexplained phenomena and ancient mysteries of the Grand Canyon, featuring interviews with experts and dramatic recreations of critical discoveries.

Appendices and Resources

- **Appendix A: Deciphering Documents and Testimonies**
  An appendix contains translated texts and interpretations of the ancient symbols and languages in the Grand Canyon.
- **Appendix B: Illustrations and Insights from the Grand Canyon**
  Detailed illustrations of the petroglyphs, hieroglyphs, and artifacts uncovered during various expeditions, accompanied by expert analyses.

Further Reading

- **The Occult and Esoteric Wisdom**
  Books and articles explore the mystical and esoteric knowledge that may be connected to the ancient civilizations of the Grand Canyon.
- **Conspiracy Theories and Hidden Histories**
  Literature examining the various conspiracy theories surrounding the Grand Canyon, including the controversial claims about hidden chambers and advanced ancient technologies.

Don't miss out!

Visit the website below and you can sign up to receive emails whenever Cassiel E. Nox publishes a new book. There's no charge and no obligation.

https://books2read.com/r/B-A-NVKWB-WCDAF

Also by Cassiel E. Nox

From Roswell to Today: The Timeline of UFOs and Aliens
The Hidden Tunnels: Unraveling the Enigmatic Secrets of the Denver
Airport
Christopher Columbus: The Untold Story of Discovery and
Controversy
Hidden Depths: The Kincaid Conspiracy and The Secrets of The
Grand Canyon

Watch for more at https://my.ionos.com/domain-details/
quantumwriterverse.com.

About the Author

Cassiel E. Nox is a renowned writer whose works transcend the boundaries of science, mystery, and imagination. Known for developing intricate tales, these stories merge conspiracy theories, metaphysics, and the latest discoveries in quantum physics. The science fiction narratives are both captivating and thought-provoking. With a passion for exploring the hidden mysteries of the universe, the writing delves deep into subjects such as extraterrestrial life, ancient secret knowledge, and cryptic phenomena. Cassiel's storytelling prowess is apparent in "Hidden Depths: The Kincaid Conspiracy and The Secrets of The Grand Canyon" and "Beyond The Collider: CERN's Quantum Rift And The Mandela Effect Mystery." In these stories, the intersections of scientific experiments and anomalous collective memories, often called the Mandela Effect, are not just brought to life, but they captivate the reader, holding their attention from start to finish. The journey continues with "From Roswell to Today: The Timeline of UFOs and Aliens," an exciting exploration of historical and contemporary accounts of UFO sightings and extraterrestrial phenomena. Cassiel is working on a science-fiction series called "When Something is Nothing," which promises to expand the horizons of imagination and intrigue further. Venturing into the world of science fiction, Cassiel crafts narratives that transport readers to distant stars and futuristic societies, all while grounded in scientific plausibility and human experience. With a background steeped in academic research and a passion for unraveling conspiracies, Cassiel E. Nox remains a distinctive voice in speculative fiction, inviting audiences to question the boundaries of reality and dream beyond the known.

Read more at https://my.ionos.com/domain-details/ quantumwriterverse.com.